Blessed

FIRST RECONCILIATION

Be Bold. Be Catholic.

My name is

I am blessed, and God made me wonderfully
and marvelously in his own image.
Jesus wants me to become
the-best-version-of-myself,
grow in virtue, and live a holy life.

On this date

Jesus is going to forgive all of my sins
during my First Reconciliation.
I am truly blessed.

Table of Contents

Session 1: You Are Blessed!   1

Opening Prayer

Welcome

Count Your Blessings

My Journey with God

From the Bible: Gratitude

I Am Blessed. I Am Grateful.

Sharing Your Blessings

Show What You Know

Journal with Jesus

Closing Prayer

Session 2: The-Best-Version-of-Yourself   31

Opening Prayer

Happiness and Free Will

Making Decisions

The Greatest Commandment

Temptation, Sin, and Grace

From the Bible: Adam and Eve

Follow Your Conscience

Show What You Know

Journal with Jesus

Closing Prayer

Session 3: God Sent Jesus to Save Us   69

Opening Prayer

The Mess

Jesus' Birth and Childhood

Jesus' Ministry

The Cross, Resurrection, and Ascension

From the Bible: Pentecost

You and the Church

Show What You Know

Journal with Jesus

Closing Prayer

Session 4: Forgiveness & Healing   105

Opening Prayer

God Loves Healthy Relationships

Forgiveness

What Is a Sacrament?

What Is Reconciliation?

From the Bible: Our Father

God Will Always Love You

Show What You Know

Journal with Jesus

Closing Prayer

Session 5: Your First Reconciliation   137

Opening Prayer

Great Moments in Life

The Garden of Your Heart

Preparation Matters

The Five Steps

From the Bible: The Prodigal Son

First, but Not Last

Show What You Know

Journal with Jesus

Closing Prayer

Session 6: It's Only the Beginning 177

Opening Prayer

So Much to Look Forward To

The Will of God and Happiness

The Prayer Process

The Power of Great Habits

From the Bible: Jesus Went to a Quiet Place

Be Grateful

Show What You Know

Journal with Jesus

Closing Prayer

My Little Catechism 203

Acknowledgments 238

Welcome!

One of the most incredible gifts God has given us as human beings is the ability to dream. Unlike any other creature, we can look into the future, imagine something bigger and better, and then come back into the present and work to bring about that richly imagined better future.

Imagine how the Church would be different if children, teenagers, and young adults wanted to attend Mass each Sunday. Imagine how the Church would be different if every Catholic in America had a dynamic personal relationship with God, went to Reconciliation regularly, and made daily prayer a touchstone in their lives. Preparation for First Reconciliation presents the perfect opportunity to turn this dream into a reality.

Catechesis is the Church's efforts to bring to life the teachings of Jesus Christ in the lives of ordinary men, women, and children. Religious education classes are one of the primary forms of catechesis.

But evangelization precedes catechesis.

Evangelization is first and foremost a dialogue. It is not a monologue. Evangelization is a personal and powerful conversation that leads to conversion of heart, mind, and soul.

And let's face it, our young people need to encounter the living God. They need to hear the Gospel in a way that is personal, intriguing, relevant, compelling, and attractive. They need to know that they are not alone in the journey of life, they need to know that they are blessed to be sons or daughters of a great King, and they need to know that God will never abandon them.

It is our hope that this program will not only prepare young Catholics for the Sacrament of Reconciliation in a dynamic way, but that it will inspire them to become lifelong Catholics.

These materials are the result of thousands of hours of rigorous research, development, and testing. More than 500 people have been involved in the process. Throughout the development of the program, students, catechists, teachers, DREs, parents, and pastors have told us what is working and what isn't. Over and over, we have refined our offering based on their feedback.

And we are not finished yet. For decades, children have been using programs that were developed once and never changed, or changed every seven years. This won't be the case with *Blessed*. We hope you provide feedback so that we can continue to improve this offering regularly.

Thank you for being part of this journey. We realize that the role you play in preparing young Catholics for First Reconciliation may be a thankless one—so we want to say thank you. Thank you for everything that you are doing for the Church. It is our hope and prayer that the program will make your experience with today's young Catholics deeply fulfilling for you and for them.

There are moments when a child's eyes become wide with excitement and begin to sparkle. At Dynamic Catholic we refer to this as the "I get it now" moment. May our efforts combined with your dedication produce more "I get it now" moments in the eyes of your students this year!

May the grace of our abundantly generous God inspire you and give you courage, wisdom, and patience.

The Dynamic Catholic Team

the
Dynamic
Catholic
Approach

Blessed *is different. One look at the materials and that is clear. It looks different and feels different because it is different. The way we developed the program is very different from how Catholic programs have been developed in the past. Backed by rigorous research and testing,* Blessed *has harnessed the latest and most effective technology in the world to create an unforgettable experience.*

Blessed *isn't different just for the sake of being different. The old way just isn't working. Eighty-five percent of young Catholics stop practicing their faith within ten years of their Confirmation. The stakes are too high. Different is needed.*

The Process

What do you remember about your First Reconciliation? Most people can't remember anything. Together we can change that for the next generation of Catholics.

There are many programs that faithfully present the teachings of the Church. But that alone is not enough. While presenting the Church's teachings faithfully is essential, it is also critical that they be presented in ways that are engaging, accessible, and relevant.

So we set out to create the very best First Reconciliation program in the world—the most dynamic program to prepare children for this great Catholic Moment. As a result, *Blessed* has taken more than three years to develop. This is what it took to create the world-class program you now hold in your hands.

YEAR ONE: LISTEN

We spent an entire year just listening: meetings—hundreds of meetings—focus groups, and phone calls. Catechists, teachers, parents, DREs, and priests told us they wanted engaging work-books, catechist-friendly leader guides, resources that draw the parents into the process, and powerful music. They told us it would be nice if for once, our Catholic materials were as good as the secular programs our children experience every day. But most of all they wanted programs that help their children dis-cover the genius of Catholicism in a way that inspires them to become lifelong Catholics.

YEAR TWO: EXPLORE

We spent the second year exploring every First Reconciliation preparation program that was currently available. We analyzed the differences and similarities among these programs. We in-vestigated which parts of each were effective and which aspects simply weren't working. We also explored best practices among other Christian churches and groups to discover how they were engaging their students. Then we spent a lot of time asking why: Why does this work? Why doesn't this work? Why don't children respond to this or that? And finally we asked: What will it take to really engage them in a meaningful discussion about the genius of Catholicism?

By the third year we were developing our own program based on what we had learned. This began a cycle of developing and testing. We would develop snippets of material and then test them with experts. A lot of the material worked, but some of it didn't. And all of it was improved by the feedback we got during testing.

Now it is time to share *Blessed* with the world. But we see this as a larger pilot study. We know it isn't perfect; no program is. The difference is, we are not done yet. Many programs get launched and are never changed. But we are excited to continuously improve this program based on the feedback you and your children provide to us. So if you see a typo or a substantial way to improve this program, please let us know.

The Experience

Blessed is a Dynamic Catholic experience designed to prepare young Catholics for the Sacrament of Reconciliation.

At the heart of the program are 42 short animated films, which range in length from 2 to 12 minutes.

Here is a quick look at the different ways *Blessed* can be experienced:

1. **Online**: The entire program will be available online to anyone at any time.

2. **Hard Copies**: The workbook, leader guide, and DVD series will also be available as hard copies for parishes and individuals who prefer them.

3. **Audiobook**: For any Catholic in America to experience the universally informative and inspiring content of *Blessed*, it is perfect for parents and loved ones of those preparing for the Sacrament.

4. **Music CD**: Catchy and inspiring music for use in the car, classroom, and home.

5. **Content in Spanish**: The entire program will also be available in Spanish.

Children ...

○ Have great differences in size and abilities

○ Love talking, often exaggerating stories

○ Work hard to please parents, catechists, teachers, and other adults

○ Thrive with structure and routine

○ Are sensitive to adult assessment

○ Compare themselves to others

○ Place high importance on friendships

○ View things as right or wrong, wonderful or terrible, with very little middle ground or gray area

○ Are beginning to use logical reasoning

○ Have a tendency to make decisions based on influence of others

○ Have difficulty with abstract reasoning

○ Need closure and desire to finish assignments

○ Want work to be perfect, erasing constantly

○ Desire to work slowly

○ Collect and organize things

○ Learn best when they feel an emotional connection

○ Have a strong sense of wonder

*Typically, children receive the Sacraments of First Reconciliation and First Communion in the second grade. But, we think you will agree, *Blessed* is for every Catholic in America.

The Elements

At Dynamic Catholic we believe everything we do as Catholics should be excellent. That's why we have sought out the best resources in the world to create an unforgettable experience with the genius of Catholicism.

THE WORKBOOKS

The beautifully illustrated workbooks are made up of more than 250 hand-painted works of art by an internationally acclaimed artist. The combination of rich visuals and dynamic content brings the faith to life for children more than ever before. The content meets children where they are and leads them step-by-step to where God is calling them to be.

THE PARENT COMPONENT

The *Blessed* parent email program, audiobook, and music CD are an answer to what catechists, teachers, DREs, priests, and Bishops have been crying out for—a dynamic way to engage disengaged parents and encourage them to make faith a priority in their lives.

THE ANIMATION

Our research revealed that cognitive retention in children from ages 6 to 9 is directly linked to emotional connection, and nothing connects with children on a significant emotional level quite like animation. So we thought it was time for Catholics to harness the techniques Disney has been using for more than ninety years to influence our children.

We teamed up with an Emmy Award–winning animation studio to create the first ever animated film series for sacramental preparation. Each of the 42 episodes will engage your children's sense of wonder and take them on an unforgettable adventure into the story of Jesus and the life-giving truths of his Church.

The Format

This program is divided into six sessions. Each session has at least 60 minutes of classroom material that can be utilized as a catechist sees fit for a particular group of students. The sessions are broken up in a way that the content can be shortened per class over a longer period of time or lengthened over a shorter period of time.

> **Our research revealed that cognitive retention in children from ages 6 to 9 is directly linked to emotional connection, and nothing connects with children on a significant emotional level quite like animation.**

THE SESSIONS

Each of the six sessions in *Blessed* have many layers. As you plan out your teaching time, look ahead, and plan for this type of structure:

1 **Opening Prayer**

2 **Teachable Moments**: Sessions 2, 3, 4, and 6 are the sessions with the primary teaching content.

3 **From the Bible**: Every session five will utilize Holy Scripture to illustrate the primary point of the session. This will help Scripture come to life!

4 **Show What You Know**: Here is an opportunity for students to answer true-or-false and fill-in-the-blank questions so you can gauge how well they are grasping the material.

5 **Journal with Jesus**: This is a prayerful opportunity for students to have an intimate conversation with Jesus. They can write or draw their thoughts to Jesus.

6 **Closing Prayer**

Additionally, there are two features intended to streamline and enhance the teaching experience:

1. Every spread has a step-by-step list of instructions and activities.

2. The page numbers correspond with the student workbook so the two books match one another.

TIPS

Throughout this leader guide, you will find a variety of tips. We recommend you read all of the tips through, start to finish. This will give you a good sense of how to engage these young Catholics in a dynamic experience. It will also give you confidence and allow you to enjoy the process—and the more you enjoy it, the more they enjoy it! Remember, you are offering them something beautiful. Give them a beautiful encounter with God and his Church and you will change their lives forever. Don't lose sight of that.

Prayer Icon: Indicates a moment when you are encouraged to pray with the children.

 Read and Explore: Indicates a suggested time for children to explore the workbooks and for the material to be read aloud, with a partner, and/or silently.

 Watch and Discuss: Indicates a time to watch one, two, or sometimes even three episodes, followed by discussion.

 Show What You Know: Indicates when children are asked to complete true-or-false and fill-in-the-blank activities.

 Journal with Jesus: Indicates the time when students engage in a personal, guided conversation with Jesus.

 Time Icon: Indicates a guide to help you plan approximately how long each activity will take.

QUOTES

Throughout this book there are quotes from some of the great Christian spiritual champions. May their words provide you with tremendous encouragement and wisdom throughout the process and, most of all, may they inspire you to become the-best-version-of-yourself, grow in virtue, and live a holy life.

Suggested Formats

One of the great challenges in developing First Reconciliation materials is that each diocese prepares candidates in different ways for different periods of time, with different class formats. With this in mind, we have developed *Blessed* with a suggested format, but in a way that makes it infinitely flexible.

We suggest that the program be experienced through six ninety-minute classes. These can take place once a month for six months, twice a month for three months, or once a week for six weeks.

If this is not how you currently structure First Reconciliation preparation, we invite you to consider trying something new. Just because you have always done it a certain way doesn't mean you need to continue to do it a certain way—especially if that way isn't producing results.

Other Formats

The core of the program is 42 short animated episodes. In the suggested format, children would experience seven of these short episodes in each class. But you could use one per class for 42 sessions, two per class for twenty-one sessions, or three per class for fourteen sessions.

The program was specifically designed to have this flexibility. Each short episode is content and concept rich. This leads to great opportunities for class or small-group discussions.

Children at this age crave repetition. For those parishes and schools that have longer programs and need more material, don't be afraid to identify key episodes and show them multiple times. There will be certain episodes that the children will gravitate toward; let those episodes and their themes become part of the fabric of the class and ultimately part of the fabric of their lives.

We Are Praying for You

In Mark's Gospel, just after the Transfiguration, Jesus comes down the mountain with Peter, James, and John. Waiting for Jesus is a father desperate for his son to be healed. The father is a bit frustrated because Jesus' disciples have been unable to rid his son of the demon that plagues him. Jesus rebukes the unclean spirit and it leaves the boy. His disciples, no doubt frustrated by their inability to cure the boy, ask Jesus, "Why could we not cast it out?" Jesus answers them, "This kind can come out only through prayer and fasting" (Mark 9:29).

Some things are so important they need prayer and fasting. In addition to creating *Blessed* we have been praying and fasting for you and the children who will experience this program. Together, with the grace of God, we will transform the hearts of all the children who experience *Blessed*, helping them become all God created them to be.

If there is anything Dynamic Catholic can ever do to serve you, please reach out to our Mission Team at 859-980-7900 or email us at blessed@dynamiccatholic.com.

In addition to creating *Blessed*, we have been praying and fasting for you and the children who will experience this program.

1

You Are Blessed!

QUICK SESSION OVERVIEW

Opening Prayer. . . . . 5 min

Watch and Discuss; Read and Explore . . . . 68 min

Show What You Know . . . . 10 min

Journal with Jesus. . . . . 5 min

Closing Prayer. . . . . 2 min

OBJECTIVES

- **TO DEMONSTRATE** to the children in your class
  that they are blessed.

- **TO EXPLAIN** to the children that First Reconciliation
  is one of many great moments in our journey with God.

- **TO TEACH** the children how to be grateful
  and how to share their blessings with others.

- # You care about your students.

- # You are excited to be on the journey toward their First Reconciliation.

1 WELCOME

Introduce yourself. Tell them a few things about you and your life—where you grew up, what football team you support, your hobbies, your favorite flavor of ice cream, and why you decided to be here right now.

Tell them this is the start of a great journey, a journey you feel blessed to be a part of.

Take a few minutes and go around the class, asking each person to say his or her name and favorite color. Many of the children may not know one another. Getting to know each other's names will help to start friendships.

Let them know you are praying for them. Encourage them to start praying for each other.

And remember what Theodore Roosevelt wrote: "People don't care how much you know, until they know how much you care."

Prayer Icon

Read and Explore

Watch and Discuss

Show What You Know

Journal with Jesus

Time Tracker

OPENING PRAYER

Step-by-Step

1 Make the Sign of the Cross together, and read the opening prayer out loud to your class.

2 Encourage and allow time for exploration. Give them a chance to dive into the book.

3 Have your students turn to the "My name is" page at the beginning of the book and fill out their name and date of their First Reconciliation. It's important for them to feel like this is a special book, just for them. The children will follow your lead. If you make it a big deal, so will they!

Nobody knows exactly what they are doing, but if you act like you do, people will think you do. Even the greatest leaders will tell you this is true.

Decision Point

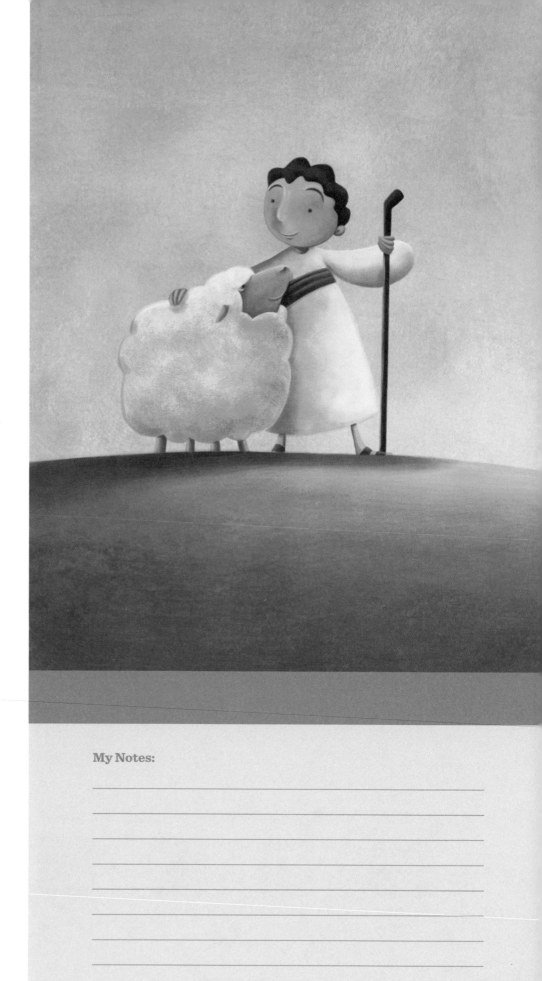

My Notes:

_____

_____

_____

_____

_____

_____

_____

1

You Are Blessed!

God, our loving Father,
thank you for all the ways you bless me.
Help me to be aware that every person,
place, and adventure I experience is an
opportunity to love you more.
Fill me with a desire to change and to grow,
and give me the wisdom to choose
the-best-version-of-myself in
every moment of every day.

Amen.

🕐
5 minutes

tip
What an awesome
opportunity this is to share
your faith with young
people! Gather everyone
for prayer. Each time you
pray, encourage everyone
to be quiet and respectful
of the time for prayer.
Utilize silence to create
a prayerful moment.
Make the Sign of the Cross
with reverence. Remember
your students are watching
you and want to follow
your example.

**The future is in
your hearts and in
your hands. God is
entrusting you the
task, at once difficult
and uplifting, of
working with him in
the building up the
civilizations of love.**

St. John Paul II

WATCH AND DISCUSS

Step-by-Step

1 Introduce the first episode. Tell the children you are excited for them to meet Ben, Sarah, and their pet gerbil, Hemingway.

2 Watch Episode 1.

3 Explore the illustration. Ask the students: "Who is the King in this picture?"
- GOD

"What is his family called?"
- THE CATHOLIC CHURCH

Young people want to be loved, not because of how they look or what they can do for another person, but simply for who they are. That is how God loves us. Our yearnings to be loved are a yearning for God.

Decision Point

Welcome

Welcome. We are beginning a great journey!

You are a child of God. You are part of the largest and most famous family in the world: the Catholic Church. You are blessed.

God wants you to always feel welcome in his presence, in his Church, and as a member of his family.

You are the son or daughter of a great King.

You may think of yourself as a boy or a girl, as young or old, as black or white, as American or Chinese, but first and foremost, you are a child of God. He is the great King, and you are his son or daughter. We all have this in common. God is our Father.

My Notes:

_____

_____

_____

_____

_____

_____

_____

7 minutes

tip
This is the first animated episode they are going to experience in the program. Make sure everyone can see the screen. Share your excitement about watching an episode for the first time with them. If you are excited to watch, they will be too!

The day you learn to surrender yourself totally to God, you will discover a new world . . . You will enjoy a peace and a calm unknown, surpassing even the happiest days of your life.

Blessed Jaime Hilario

3

READ AND EXPLORE

Step-by-Step

1 Read this section out loud to your students.

2 Share with the students some of the best gifts you have ever received. Try not to focus on material blessings. Instead, focus on blessings that often go unnoticed.

Examples:

- AIR TO BREATHE
- EARS TO LISTEN
- A FAVORITE MEAL
- SUNSETS
- FAMILY
- AND THE GREATEST GIFT OF ALL, LIFE

Without gratitude, what was extraordinary yesterday becomes ordinary today.

Rediscover Jesus

4

You Are Blessed

You are blessed. What does it mean to be blessed? It means that God loves you and showers you with gifts.

You are blessed in so many ways, but every blessing you experience flows from the first blessing. You are a child of God. This is the original blessing.

What's the best gift you have ever received?

My Notes:

_____

_____

_____

_____

_____

_____

_____

You may think it is a bike, a baseball bat, a dress, a bracelet, or a video game. But this is not true.

The best gift you have ever received is LIFE. Life makes every other gift possible. Without life, you wouldn't be able to enjoy any other gift!

This is just one of a thousand reasons why life is sacred. God loves life.

The very first thing we read about in the Bible is how God created everything. Then God looked at all he had created and said, "It is good" (Genesis 1:31).

You are blessed in so many ways, but every blessing flows from the blessing of life.

You may be blessed to run like the wind, but if God had not given you life, you wouldn't be able to do that. You may be blessed to eat ice cream, but only because God gave you the original blessing.

You may be blessed to sing like an angel, but only because God gave you life first.

God has given you life and made you his child. You are blessed.

5 minutes

tip

To successfully lead, you have to see your students as real people, and they have to see you as a real person. One of the most powerful tools you have to lead this group is your story. Feel free to share things about yourself as you spend time with the class to cultivate trust and honesty with them.

God has sent you as workers into his harvest that through your ministry, faith may be preserved and love may grow.

St. Vincent Pallotti

WATCH AND DISCUSS

Step-by-Step

1 Introduce Episode 2 by saying: "We are blessed in so many ways, but Ben and Sarah are going to share the greatest blessing of all!"

2 Watch Episodes 2 and 3

3 Ask the students: "Can you name the blessings in your life?" Write these blessings on the board. Keep going until the children have named a total of 50 blessings.

If they get stuck, suggest:

life, family, friends, school, a favorite toy, food, a favorite sport, music or an instrument, good health, a favorite pet, the Earth, being healthy, Summer vacation, Christmas, Easter, a comfy bed, America, and God

Count Your Blessings

There is an ancient Jewish saying, "Count your blessings!" Jewish rabbis encourage their people to count their blessings each day and see if they can get to one hundred.

Counting our blessings leads us to gratitude. When we count our blessings, we become full of joy and gratitude. God loves a grateful heart. As children of God we should try to begin and end each day with gratitude.

God blesses us in lots of ways. When we count our blessings we are really saying THANK YOU to God for all the fabulous talents, things, people, experiences, and opportunities he gives us.

My Notes:

_____

_____

_____

_____

_____

_____

_____

When someone asks, "How are you?" rather than just saying "good" or "fine," you can say, "I am blessed!" It helps us to remember this, and it reminds others that they are blessed, too.

What are some of the ways God has blessed you?

15 minutes

tip

One of the most powerful habits for a young person is to develop an attitude of gratitude. Counting blessings leads to gratitude. From time to time, have your children count their blessings.

Be faithful in small things because it is in them that your strength lies.

St. Teresa of Calcutta

READ AND EXPLORE

Step-by-Step

1 Have the children fill out the Gratitude List. If they have a hard time, refer to the list on the board that the class made together. Be sure they spend no more than 5 minutes filling out their list.

> Gratitude reminds us of what matters most and what matters least, and fills us with resolve to carry on the great mission God has entrusted to us.
>
> Resisting Happiness

My Gratitude List

I am grateful for . . .

_____

_____

_____

_____

_____

_____

My Notes:

_____

_____

_____

_____

_____

_____

5 minutes

tip

Your students should continue to add to the Gratitude List in the workbook throughout the course of their preparation. Any time they want to add something to the list, encourage them to share with the class.

For those who love, nothing is too difficult, especially when it is done for the love of our Lord Jesus Christ.

St. Ignatius of Loyola

WATCH AND DISCUSS

Step-by-Step

1 Introduce Episode 4 by saying: "In this episode, Fr. Tom shares some of the great moments in his life."

2 Watch Episode 4.

3 Activity:

I KNOW MY NEIGHBOR
Have a volunteer be "it." Have everyone else stand in a circle with the volunteer in the middle. The volunteer will say, "I know my neighbor who..." and something like: "is wearing jeans" or "plays a sport." If the statement is true for a student, he or she must move to a new spot in the circle. Students for whom the statement does not apply will stay where they are. The volunteer also has to find a place in the circle. There will be one fewer spot than there are players, so the person without a spot is "it" for the next round. Continue for five minutes or until everyone has been "it."

My Journey with God

We are all children of God. This makes us all much more alike than we are different. Too often we focus on our differences rather than remembering that we are all brothers and sisters, that we are all children of the same great King.

God gave you life, and he has designed a great journey just for you. Along the way there are going to be some very important moments in your journey.

My Notes:

_____

_____

_____

_____

_____

_____

_____

_____

Baptism

First, there was your Baptism, which was the beginning of your new life in Jesus. This is when you became a member of his Church and joined the largest and most famous family in the world, the Catholic Church.

When and where were you baptized?

12 minutes

tip

If you are following the suggested 90-minute format, this marks the approximate halfway point. It is a good time for a brief break. If you are running behind, take a quick look ahead and see where you can get back on track. If ahead of schedule, look for an opportunity in the next 45 minutes to spark a great conversation. If on time, press on and finish strong!

_____

_____

_____

_____

_____

_____

For although he is right with us and in and out of us and all through us, we have to go on journeys to find him.

Thomas Merton

11

READ AND EXPLORE

Step-by-Step

1 Ask your students: "When will you receive your First Reconciliation and First Communion?" Have them write their answers in the book.

It is not the magnitude of our actions but the amount of love that is put into them that matters.

St. Teresa of Calcutta

First Reconciliation

Now, you are preparing for your First Reconciliation. We all mess up from time to time. We all do things that offend God and place obstacles between him and us. When we get separated from God we become unhappy. Reconciliation removes these obstacles and fills our hearts and souls with joy again.

When will you receive the blessing of your First Reconciliation? I will receive my First Reconciliation on...

My Notes:

_____

_____

_____

_____

_____

_____

_____

First Communion

Before too long, the blessing of Reconciliation will prepare you for your First Communion. Receiving Jesus in the Eucharist is one of the greatest blessings of our lives.

When will you receive Jesus in the Eucharist for the first time? I will receive my First Communion on...

Confirmation

When you are a little older, you will be blessed again when you receive the Sacrament of Confirmation. Confirmation reminds us that in Baptism, God blessed us with a special mission and filled us with the Holy Spirit. It reminds us of these incredible blessings and gives us the courage and wisdom to live out the mission God has given us.

2 minutes

READ AND EXPLORE

Step-by-Step

1 Ask your students to name anyone they know who has received the Sacraments of Marriage or Holy Orders.

For example:

- THEIR PARENTS OR GRANDPARENTS FOR THE SACRAMENT OF MARRIAGE
- THE PARISH PRIEST OR DEACON FOR THE SACRAMENT OF HOLY ORDERS

Never instill a fear of defeat in a child. A Christian must be able to respond to times of defeat and thrive again.

Mustard Seeds

Marriage

Later in life, God may bless you again with Marriage or Holy Orders. In the Sacrament of Marriage, God brings a man and woman together to cherish each other, to live a holy life together, and to help each other become the-best-version-of-themselves, grow in virtue, and get to heaven.

Holy Orders

God calls some people to become priests, deacons, and bishops through the Sacrament of Holy Orders.

Anointing Of The Sick

If along your journey you get sick and need God's healing for body, mind, or spirit, you will be blessed with the Anointing of the Sick.

My Notes:

_____

_____

_____

_____

_____

_____

_____

_____

_____

You are on a great journey with God. Along the way you will experience these great Catholic Moments, which we call the Seven Sacraments. Each of these Moments is a blessing. They are all connected. These great Moments are designed by God to help you live a good life here on earth, and they prepare you to live with God in heaven forever.

You are blessed.

2 minutes

tip

Speak up! Remember young people can be slow to participate, so it might be helpful if you are ready with some of your own answers to offer too.

And we know that in all things God works for the good of those who love him, who have been called according to his purpose.

Romans 8:28

WATCH AND DISCUSS

Step-by-Step

1 Introduce the video: "The next video is about gratitude. After the video, I will tell you about a time when I was particularly thankful for a blessing from God."

2 Watch Episode 5.

3 Share with your students a time when you were particularly thankful for a blessing from God. This could be about a big moment in your life, like having your first child, or it could be a smaller moment, like watching a beautiful sunset.

By transforming the activities of our days into prayer, we put God at the center of everything we do.

Mustard Seeds

My Notes:

_____

_____

_____

_____

_____

_____

_____

_____

From the Bible: Gratitude

When we take time to pray, reflect, and count our blessings, we realize that God has blessed us in so many ways. Gratitude is the best response to any blessing. There is a wonderful story in the Gospel of Luke about gratitude.

One day while Jesus was traveling to Jerusalem, ten men with leprosy approached him and asked him to cure them. Most people would not go anywhere near a person with leprosy because the disease is very contagious, but Jesus had mercy on them.

He blessed them and said, "Go and show yourselves to the priests." Along the way, the lepers realized that they had been healed. It was a miracle!

When one of the lepers saw that he was cured of this horrible disease, he was filled with joy and immediately went back to Jesus and praised him at the top of his voice. Jesus asked the man, "Where are the others?"

Adapted from Luke 17:11–19

5 minutes

tip

The fifth episode in every session of this workbook is a story from the Bible. Why? 50 years of research shows that children thrive on routine. Our own research at Dynamic Catholic shows that making strong connections between the stories in the Bible and everyday life is critical if we want Catholics to become life-long readers of the Scriptures. Nothing about *Blessed* is random or accidental. Every part of this program is designed to drive desired outcomes. Take your time with these Bible passages. Read them slowly, as if nobody has ever heard them before. One of the ways we respect the Word of God is simply in the way we read it. Remind the students that the Bible is a great way to learn valuable life lessons and grow closer to God. Share with the class that you wish you had immersed yourself in the wisdom of the Bible much earlier in your life.

Love God, serve God; everything is in that.

St. Clare of Assisi

17

READ AND EXPLORE

Step-by-Step

1 Read aloud the lessons the one leper who came back teaches us.

2 Ask the students: "If you were one of the lepers, how would you feel after Jesus healed you?"

You can answer by suggesting feelings like:

- THANKFUL
- HAPPY
- EXCITED
- RELIEVED

Being a Christian is not about being perfect. Membership among the followers of Jesus Christ does not require perfection. But it does require us to live as Jesus invites us to live.

Rediscover Jesus

Jesus had cured all ten lepers, but only one said thank you. Jesus had just changed their lives forever, but they couldn't even be bothered to come back and say thank you. That's rude, don't you think?

Perhaps the others intended to thank Jesus, but they got distracted with life. Maybe they thought to themselves, "I will thank Jesus tomorrow, or next week."

The one leper who came back teaches us many lessons.

1. Be grateful when God blesses you.

2. It's rude not to be grateful.

3. When God blesses you abundantly, say thank you in a big way. The leper who did come back didn't just whisper thank you into Jesus' ear. He praised Jesus at the top of his voice.

4. Don't put off important things. That includes your daily prayer and going to church. When did the one leper go back and thank Jesus? Immediately. He didn't put it off.

5. When we acknowledge God's blessings we become filled with joy.

Every person in every Bible story has a lesson to teach you. Each Sunday at Mass, think about the people in the readings and what lesson God is trying to teach you through their lives.

My Notes:

_____

_____

_____

_____

_____

_____

_____

3 minutes

tip

Don't be afraid of silence. After you ask a question, anticipate a pause of several seconds. Some people need longer than others to process. That's OK. You can always come back to someone who needs more time. "I can see that you are working on your answer. I'll give you a moment." OR "Would you like me to come back to you?"

It is not fitting, when one is in God's service, to have a gloomy face or a chilling look.

St. Francis of Assisi

READ AND EXPLORE

Step-by-Step

1 Read the text to the class.

2 Ask your class: "Why was it rude for the other lepers to not return to thank Jesus?"

- JESUS BLESSED THE LEPERS BY HEALING THEM. EVERY TIME WE RECEIVE A GIFT FROM GOD WE SHOULD SAY THANK YOU!

How well do you know the story of Jesus Christ? It is the most powerful story ever told. But it loses its power when we become so familiar with it that we stop hearing it as part of our own story.

Rediscover Jesus

I Am Blessed. I Am Grateful.

One of the ways we can love God is by being grateful for all the ways he has blessed us. God blesses us in a thousand ways every day. But often we take these blessings for granted.

Can you see? You are blessed! Imagine what it is like to be blind. Everyday you look at a thousand things, but when is the last time you thanked God for giving you sight? Sight is an incredible blessing, but we often take it for granted. You are blessed! If you can read, you are blessed! If you are not in bed sick, you are blessed! If you have people who care about you, you are blessed! If you are receiving an education and learning to love learning, you are blessed! If someone in your life loves you so much that they want you to learn about God and his Church, you are blessed! If you have clean water to drink, food to eat, and a place to sleep, you are blessed! If you live in a country where there is liberty and justice, you are blessed!

The list goes on and on. You are blessed!

My Notes:

_____

_____

_____

_____

_____

_____

_____

_____

God is blessing you every day in a thousand ways. Some of these blessings you may take for granted because he gives them to you so often, such as air to breathe, water to drink, food to eat, and a bed to sleep in! This is why it is important to take time each day to count our blessings.

The perfect response to God's blessings has two parts: First, be grateful; second, share your blessings with others.

Just like the leper who returned to praise Jesus at the top of his voice, we too should express our gratitude to God for all his blessings.

5 minutes

tip

Be sure to compliment your children. When you do, be specific and honest. Why? Because children are often smarter and more perceptive than we give them credit for. They can detect false praise from a mile away, and the second they detect false praise, you lose credibility. Being honest allows you to come across as sincere, and your students will appreciate it. When you are specific, it lets the children know that you are really taking notice of them, and it will encourage them to become the-best--version-of-themselves. After all, we all shine when we realize that someone cares enough to notice.

The secret of happiness is to live moment by moment and to thank God for all that He, in His goodness, sends to us day after day.

St. Gianna Molla

21

WATCH AND DISCUSS

Step-by-Step

1 Introduce Episode 6 by saying: "In this episode Ben brings flowers to thank Sr. Rosa for being such an amazing teacher. As you watch, think about one thing you can do to bless someone in your life."

2 Watch Episodes 6.

3 Ask the children, "What is one thing you can do to bless someone in your life?"

- LISTEN TO YOUR PARENTS BY GOING TO BED WHEN YOU ARE TOLD.
- SHARE YOUR TOYS WITH YOUR SIBLINGS.
- SAY THANK YOU TO YOUR TEACHERS.

Jesus wants you to astonish people with your generosity.

Rediscover Jesus

22

Sharing Your Blessings

The second way to respond perfectly to God's blessings is to share the blessings. God blesses you so that you can bless others! There are more ways for you to bless others than there are stars in the sky. You can bless someone by helping him with something. You can bless someone by listening to what she has to say. You can bless your parents by living a good life. That's right! Good children are a great blessing to their parents. You can bless someone by encouraging him to continue when he wants to give up. You can bless someone by praying for her and asking God to watch over her. You can bless someone by helping him become the-best-version-of-himself.

My Notes:

_____

_____

_____

_____

_____

_____

_____

Few things in life will bring you more joy than sharing God's blessings with others. But in order to share your blessings with others, you need to be very clear about one thing: you are blessed!

So when you lay your head on your pillow tonight, whisper quietly, "I am blessed. Thank you, God, for blessing me today. I am blessed."

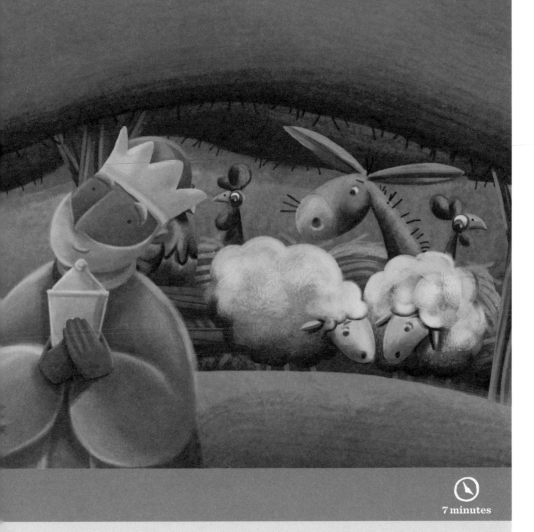

7 minutes

Follow your star. Wait for it to rise, and while you are waiting, prepare yourself. Become infinitely familiar with your needs, talents, and desires. Remember, circumstances, whether they appear to be good or bad, are opportunities. When you see a star rise on the horizon of your life and you are filled with a burning desire to follow it, and you perceive that by following it you will use your talents and fulfill your legitimate needs—follow it.

Matthew Kelly

23

Step-by-Step

1. Have students complete the activity page by themselves, with a partner, or together as a class.

2. After 5 minutes ask the class, "Are there any questions you are struggling with?

3. Briefly explain the answer to each question they have by referring back to the section in the workbook that relates to it.

Some things are important. But, no thing is more important than someone. For everyone is a child of God.

Decision Point

Show What You Know

True or False

1. __T__ You are on a great journey with God. (p 10)

2. __F__ You have nothing to be grateful for. (p 17)

3. __F__ Gratitude is the worst response to any blessing. (p 17)

4. __T__ God wants you to become the-best-version-of-yourself. (p 22)

5. __T__ God loves a grateful heart. (p 6)

Fill in the blank

1. The greatest blessing God has ever given you is _____**life**_____. (p 5)

2. When we count our blessings, we become full of __**gratitude**__ and _____**joy**_____. (p 6)

3. The _____**Catholic Church**_____ is the largest and most famous family in the world. (p 2)

4. _____**Baptism**_____ is the beginning of your new life in Jesus. (p 11)

5. _____**Confirmation**_____ reminds us that in Baptism God blessed us with a special mission and filled us with the Holy Spirit. (p 13)

My Notes:

_____

_____

_____

_____

_____

_____

_____

_____

6. You are a member of God's _____family_____. (p 2)

7. When God blesses you abundantly, say_____thank you_____ in a big way. (p 18)

8. Every person in every Bible story has a _____lesson_____ to teach you. (p 18)

9. I am_____blessed_____. (p 20)

10. God blesses you so that you can _____bless_____ others. (p 22)

Word Bank

CONFIRMATION	LIFE	JOY	THANK YOU	BLESSED	FAMILY
CATHOLIC CHURCH	BAPTISM	BLESS	GRATITUDE	LESSON	

10 minutes

tip

If you are running short on time, you may choose to complete this section together as a class. Simply read each fill-in-the-blank and true-or--false statement and invite your students to call out the answer. Once someone calls out the right answer, ask everyone to write it down in their workbooks. If you are completely out of time, ask the children to complete the exercise for homework.

Start children on the way they should go, and even when they are old they will not turn from it

Proverbs 22:6

JOURNAL WITH JESUS

Step By Step

1 Invite your children to write a letter to Jesus.

2 Read the journal prompt aloud.

3 Ask the class to remain silent during their journaling time.

4 You may wish to play some quiet reflective music to help create the right mood in the classroom and to encourage the students to remain quiet and focused on Journaling with Jesus

Small can triumph over big. It has before and will again. If ever things seem against you, hold your head up; persevere.

Mustard Seeds

My Notes:

_____

_____

_____

_____

_____

_____

_____

Journal with Jesus

Dear Jesus,

I am so blessed because . . .

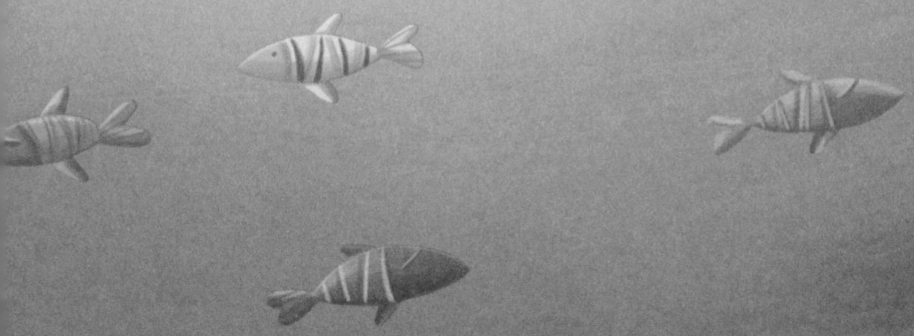

5 minutes

tip

Christianity has always spread through witness. Teaching this program is an incredible opportunity for you to grow personally. The more you immerse yourself in *Blessed*, the more likely the young people before you will immerse themselves. Whether it is before or after class, take time and write your own letter to Jesus. It doesn't have to be in every class, but from time to time share with your students something you wrote to Jesus in your letter. They will learn something from what you share, but they will learn more from knowing that you are taking these exercises seriously.

Place your talents and enthusiasm at the service of life.

St. John Paul II

CLOSING PRAYER

Step-by-Step

1 Introduce Episode 7 by saying: "In this episode, Ben is going to lead us in Mary's prayer of gratitude. Let's quiet down and pay special attention to this short episode.

2 Watch Episode 7.

3 If time allows, ask the students: "What are some of the most important things you learned in this session?"

- COUNT MY BLESSINGS.
- RECONCILIATION IS A GREAT MOMENT IN MY JOURNEY WITH GOD.
- SHOW GRATITUDE TOWARD GOD.
- SHARE ALL MY BLESSINGS WITH OTHERS.
- I AM THE SON/DAUGHTER OF A GREAT KING.

Closing Prayer:

One of the most famous prayers is Mary's song of gratitude, called the Magnificat:

My soul proclaims the greatness of the Lord,
and my spirit rejoices in God my savior,
for he has looked with favor on me.
From now on all generations will call me blessed.
For the mighty one has done great things for me,
and holy is his name.

Adapted from Luke 1:46–49

This was just one of the ways Mary showed her enormous gratitude to God. You too can praise God with your gratitude, morning, noon, and night. Let's praise God right now with our own prayer:

Oh Lord my God, thank you for all the ways you have blessed me in the past, all the ways you are blessing me today, and all the ways you plan to bless me in the future.
I know you have great plans for me.
Help me never to doubt you.

Amen.

My Notes:

_____

_____

_____

_____

_____

_____

_____

2 minutes

tip

Episode 7 in every session is the closing prayer. These episodes were intentionally designed to be educational, inspirational, practical, and entertaining. Remind your students that in this episode we are not just watching Ben pray as a form of entertainment; we are actually praying with him. With that in mind, let's be sure to have the students make the Sign of the Cross at the beginning and the end of the prayer with Ben.

> **Our Lord does not so much look at the greatness of our actions, or even at their difficulty, as at the love with which we do them.**
>
> St. Thérèse de Lisieux

29

2

The-Best-Version-Of-Yourself

QUICK SESSION OVERVIEW

Opening Prayer. . . . . 2 min

Watch and Discuss; Read and Explore . . . . 70 min

Show What You Know . . . . 10 min

Journal with Jesus . . . . 5 min

Closing Prayer. . . . . 3 min

OBJECTIVES

- **TO DEMONSTRATE** that we are always happier when we follow the Ten Commandments.

- **TO EXPLAIN** that God is always willing to give us another chance and a fresh start through Reconciliation.

- **TO TEACH** that God wants us to become great decision makers.

NOTHING SAYS, "I CARE ABOUT YOU!" TO CHILDREN
QUITE LIKE A LEADER WHO . . .

- ## Says he or she is going to pray for you.

- ## Actually prays for you.

1 WELCOME

In his time on earth, Jesus led by serving. Whether it was washing the feet of his disciples, healing the sick, feeding the hungry, or giving his life on the cross, Jesus served people in powerful ways.

Jesus is asking you to lead these children by serving them. One of the most important and powerful ways you can serve is through prayer.

On the night before he died, Jesus prayed out loud. He prayed for his disciples, and he prayed for all future believers, including you and me. He prayed for unity among believers and he prayed that the Good News would be spread throughout the world.

Jesus teaches us that servant leaders pray for those entrusted to their care. You have generously accepted this opportunity to love these children, walk with them in their journey, and give them a life-changing experience with the genius of Catholicism they will never forget. You can't do this without prayer.

So, pray for your students. Pray for their families. And let your children know you are doing so. Never underestimate the power of prayer in your life, your children's lives, and the lives of their families.

Prayer Icon

Read and Explore

Watch and Discuss

Show What You Know

Journal with Jesus

Time Tracker

OPENING PRAYER

Step-by-Step

1 Introduce the opening prayer by saying: "Let's take a moment in silence to be still and quiet and open ourselves up to whatever God wants to lead us to today."

2 Make the Sign of the Cross together, deliberately. Read the opening prayer slowly and reflectively.

God lives in the eternal now. He is constantly inviting us to immerse ourselves in the present moment so we can be with him.

Resisting Happiness

My Notes:

_____

_____

_____

_____

_____

_____

_____

2

The-Best-Version-of-Yourself

God, our loving Father,
thank you for all the ways you bless me.
Help me to be aware that every person,
place, and adventure I experience is an
opportunity to love you more.
Fill me with a desire to change and to grow,
and give me the wisdom to choose
the-best-version-of-myself in
every moment of every day.

Amen.

2 minutes

tip

Use silence to your advantage. Really wait for and create silence. After twenty or thirty seconds of silence—which will seem like an eternity for them, and maybe for you—begin the prayer. You will be amazed at what a little silence can do for young people.

Mental prayer is nothing else than an intimate friendship, a frequent heart-to-heart conversation with him by whom we know ourselves to be loved.

St. Theresa of Ávila

WATCH AND DISCUSS

Step-by-Step

1 Introduce the first episode by saying: "In this episode, we will see how Max is able to become a great decision maker."

2 Watch Episode 1.

3 Ask the children: "What are some of the ways you have exercised free will this week?"

If they have trouble answering, here are some examples to help:

- HELPED MY FRIEND
- PRAYED TO GOD
- LISTENED TO MY TEACHER
- DID MY HOMEWORK
- CLEANED MY ROOM
- ATE MY VEGETABLES
- LISTENED TO MY PARENTS

Happiness and Free Will

You are blessed! One of the greatest blessings God has given you is the ability to make choices. We call this free will.

Free will is the gift God gives us to allow us to make our own choices. Each time we make a choice, God hopes we will choose what is good and right and what helps us become the-best-version-of-ourselves.

God has given you free will and he wants you to become a great decision maker. You are young and it might seem like people are always telling you what to do. But you exercise your free will in a hundred ways every day. What are some of the ways you have exercised your free will this week?

My Notes:

_____

_____

_____

_____

_____

_____

_____

God wants to teach you how to make great decisions and do the right thing because he wants you to be happy.

Doing the right thing is also one of the ways we show that we love God, others, and ourselves. God wants your love to be large and generous. He wants you to be kind, loving, thoughtful, compassionate, helpful, and accepting.

Learn to say yes with God. This means that before you say yes to anything, ask yourself: Would God want me to say yes to this? Will this help me become the-best-version-of-myself?

Learn to say no with God too. Before you say no to anything, ask yourself: Would God want me to say no to this?

Say yes with God and say no with God, and your love of God and neighbor will be large and generous. This is the path to happiness.

5 minutes

tip

tip
Trust is essential to every great relationship. In order for your children to trust you, they first need to feel safe to be themselves. When children feel safe to be themselves, they will talk freely, share their hearts, and believe what you say.

Our only desire and our one choice should be this: I want and I choose what better leads to God deepening his life in me.

St. Ignatius of Loyola

WATCH AND DISCUSS

Step-by-Step

1. Give your children a moment to explore the illustration. Encourage them to be filled with awe.

2. Introduce Episode 2 by saying: "In the next episode Ben, Sarah, and Hemingway go on a great adventure!"

3. Watch Episode 2.

In our lives there comes a time when the only thing that matters is the will of God.

Mustard Seeds

Making Decisions

One of the most practical skills you can develop in life is to become a great decision maker. King Solomon was called "Solomon the Wise" because he was a great decision maker.

Solomon was just twelve years old when he became king, and he was very nervous about how he would make all the decisions a king needs to make. One night God appeared to Solomon in a dream. He told Solomon he would give him anything he asked for. Solomon asked God for wisdom.

My Notes:

God wants you to become a great decision maker too.

We have spoken about how God wants you to become the-best-version-of-yourself and live a holy life. This is simply not possible unless you get really good at making decisions.

Remember, God doesn't expect you to become wise and learn to make great decisions all on your own. He gives you guidance. One way God guides us is by giving us laws. God gives us directions to follow, which are designed to help us live happy and holy lives by guiding us to make great decisions.

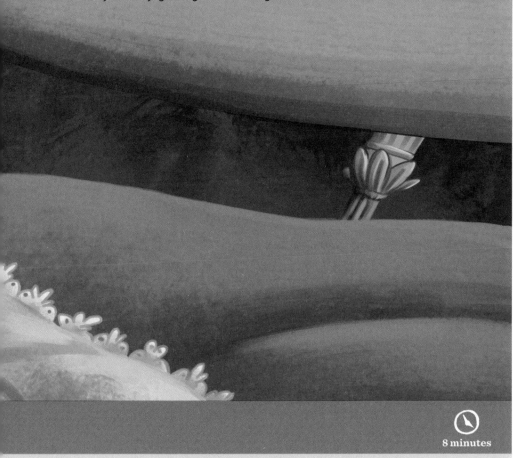

8 minutes

tip

At Dynamic Catholic we believe that children are inspired by beauty. With that in mind, we have intentionally made each illustration its own work of art. Hand-painted and hand-drawn by an internationally acclaimed children's artist, every page is intended to bring out a child's sense of wonder. As they explore each page, students might say things like "Wow!" or "I like this one!" or "This is really cool!" In these moments, don't discourage them. Encourage them. If they fall in love with the book, it will become a part of them and it will make their First Reconciliation experience unforgettable.

Ask and it will be given to you; seek and you will find; knock and the door will be opened to you

Matthew 7:7

Step-by-Step

1. Read the last paragraph out loud.

2. Emphasize to your students how God will never give up on his people and he will always give them another chance.

The Best Way to Live

Moses was a great leader chosen by God to lead the Israelites out of slavery in Egypt. The Israelites were God's chosen people, and he blessed them by taking care of them.

God helped the Israelites escape from slavery in Egypt by parting the Red Sea. When the people were hungry, he sent them special food from heaven called manna. When they were thirsty, he made water come out of a rock for them to drink. And God led them to the Promised Land, a fabulous country filled with food and fresh water, where they could all live together as an extended family.

My Notes:

_____

_____

_____

_____

_____

_____

_____

The Gospel is pure genius. It is the ultimate worldview, the most complete spiritual manual, and the best way to live.

Rediscover Jesus

But along the way, the people became restless and ungrateful, began complaining, and turned their backs on God in lots of ways. They were also arguing with each other about what was the best way to live.

And yet, God did not give up on his people. Even though they had turned their backs on him and sinned against him, and even though they were not being the-best-version-of-themselves, he gave them another chance.

2 minutes

tip

tip

Repetition is essential to learning. Take riding a bike, for example. When a child is learning to ride a bike, the more attempts he or she makes, the more the brain reinforces the particular skills necessary to stay balanced and in motion. After enough repetition, the child no longer has to stop and think about how to ride a bike. He or she just rides. Even years later, after a long absence from riding, it's possible for that person to get back on a bike and just ride. That's how powerful repetition can be.

If your children remember nothing else from their First Reconciliation experience, make sure they know this: Even if they turn their backs on him, God will never give up on them. He will never stop loving them. He will always give them another chance. Constantly ask the children, "Will God ever give up on you?" or "Will God ever stop loving you?" Encourage them to say "No!" loudly and proudly.

Effectively use repetition and the children will spend a lifetime knowing God will never forsake them.

READ AND EXPLORE

Step-by-Step

1 Ask the children: "God spoke to Moses through a burning bush—do you think he still speaks to us today?"

2 If time allows, share an experience you had when God spoke into your life.

God speaks to us all in a variety of ways. He speaks to us where we are and in a way we can understand.

Mustard Seeds

God Speaks to Moses

God invited Moses to come up a very high mountain as a representative of the people. On top of Mount Sinai he spoke to Moses through the burning bush. He also gave Moses his law written on two stone tablets—the Ten Commandments.

The Ten Commandments are a blessing from God given to his people. They help us become the-best-version-of-ourselves, grow in virtue, and live holy lives.

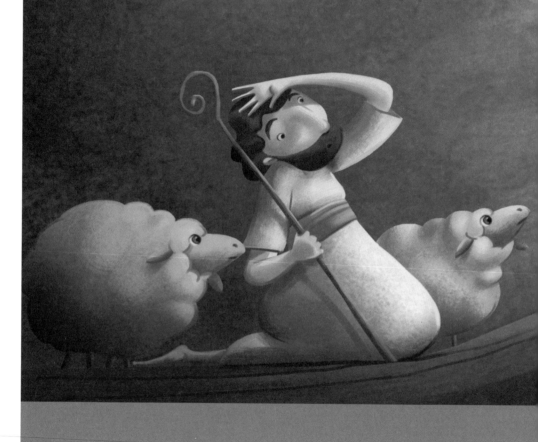

My Notes:

_____

_____

_____

_____

_____

_____

_____

5 minutes

tip

The best way to teach children is to first understand them. Children need to know that you respect and value them, which is the message they get when you take the time to talk with them, observe them, and learn about them as people. Find out their interests, temperaments, and learning styles. Discover what motivates them, how they best learn, their skills and talents, and the challenges that impact their day-to-day lives. With this knowledge you can teach children in a way that capitalizes on their strengths and builds their confidence.

It is not hard to obey when we love the one whom we obey.

St. Ignatius of Loyola

Step-by-Step

1 Ask: "Which commandment is hardest for you to keep?" If it helps, here is a different way to describe the Ten Commandments.

1. ONLY GOD CAN BE GOD.

2. IT'S ONLY OKAY TO SAY, "GOD" IF YOU ARE PRAYING. YOU SHOULD BE CAREFUL NOT TO SAY THINGS LIKE "OH MY GOD!"

3. ATTEND SUNDAY MASS.

4. LISTEN TO YOUR PARENTS, AND RESPECT ALL ADULTS.

5. RESPECT ALL LIFE.

6. KEEP YOUR PROMISES TO GOD AND ONE ANOTHER.

7. IF IT'S NOT YOURS, DON'T TAKE IT WITHOUT PERMISSION.

8. DO NOT LIE OR SAY BAD THINGS ABOUT OTHERS.

9. BE HAPPY WITH WHO YOU ARE AND WHAT YOU HAVE.

10. DO NOT BE JEALOUS OF WHAT OTHERS HAVE.

The Ten Commandments

The Ten Commandments show us the best way to live, and they are just as important today as they were thousands of years ago when Moses brought them down from Mount Sinai. They point us along the path of wisdom, and lead all of humanity toward peace, harmony, joy, and holiness.

We are always happier when we walk in God's ways. We are always happier when we obey God's laws.

What are the Ten Commandments?

1. I am the Lord your God; you shall not have strange gods before me.

2. You shall not take the name of the Lord your God in vain.

3. Remember to keep holy the Lord's Day.

4. Honor your father and mother.

5. You shall not kill.

6. You shall not commit adultery.

7. You shall not steal.

8. You shall not bear false witness against your neighbor.

9. You shall not covet your neighbor's wife.

10. You shall not covet your neighbor's goods.

Which commandment is the hardest for you to keep?

My Notes:

_____

_____

_____

_____

_____

_____

_____

_____

7 minutes

tip

Have fun! Seriously, have fun with this. Don't worry if something doesn't work out as planned. Instead, take the approach of an explorer. Try to see things as fresh and new—a great discovery! Be enthusiastic when your children share ideas, feelings, or thoughts. Children will pick up on your enthusiasm. The by-product of your enthusiasm and joy will be a group of children who fall in love with learning and appreciate the genius of Catholicism.

The world offers you comfort, but you were not made for comfort, you were made for greatness.

Pope Benedict XVI

41

WATCH AND DISCUSS

Step-by-Step

1 Introduce Episode 3 by saying: "In this episode you are going to learn why God sent Jesus to earth."

2 Watch Episode 3.

3 Ask the children: "Why did God send his Son Jesus to earth?"

If no one is able to provide an answer, encourage a student to re-read aloud: God sent his only son Jesus to save people from their sin and confusion, and show them the best way to live.

Serving others is the surest path to happiness in this world, to discovering who you are and what you are here for.

Decision Point

The Greatest Commandment

Moses lived more than one thousand years before Jesus was born. After he came down from the mountain the people tried to walk with God and live holy lives by obeying his commandments. Some days they did a great job, and other days they gave in to temptation and sin.

As the years passed, more and more of the people turned their backs on God and his law. They stopped trying to live holy lives, became confused about the best way to live, and made excuses for their behavior.

My Notes:

_____

_____

_____

_____

_____

_____

_____

But God still loved his people. So when the time was right, he sent his only son, Jesus, to save people from their sin and confusion and show them the best way to live.

One day Jesus was in the synagogue listening and teaching, when someone asked him a question: "Teacher, which is the greatest of the commandments?" Jesus replied, "You shall love the Lord your God with all your heart, with all your soul, and with all your mind. This is the greatest commandment. And the second is like it: "You shall love your neighbor as yourself" (Matthew 22:36–40).

6 minutes

tip

From time to time you will need to get your children's attention to say something important. There are many ways to do this. One great way is to establish nonverbal communication. For example, hold one hand in the air, make eye contact with your students, and wait until they raise their hands and quiet down too. Once everyone is quiet, you can lower your hand and begin talking. Another great way to get their attention is by clapping your hands three times and teaching them to clap back twice. It's fun, it gets their attention, and it lets them know you are about to say something important.

Any routine takes time and patience, but the payoff is enormous.

Charity is certainly greater than any rule. Moreover, all rules must lead to charity.

St. Vincent de Paul

Step-by-Step

1 Read the first two
paragraphs aloud.

2 Utilize call-and-response to
grab students' attention:

Call: "I will treat"

Response: I will treat

C: "others the way"

R: others the way

C: "I want to be treated"

R: I want to be treated

Love One Another

If we love God with all our hearts, souls, and minds, we will try every day to become a-better-version-of-ourselves, to live holy lives, and obey God's commandments.

Jesus wanted everyone to know that it is not enough just to say that we love God. He wanted us to know that one of the most powerful ways we show God that we love him is by loving other people. Jesus was always standing up for the people who could not stand up for themselves. And he teaches us to treat other people the way we would like to be treated.

God is constantly trying to show us the best way to live. He gave Moses the Ten Commandments to share with us so that we could live holy lives. He sent Jesus to clear the confusion about what is right and what is wrong. After Jesus died, rose from the dead, and ascended into heaven, God the Father sent the Holy Spirit to guide us. He has also given us the Bible and the One, Holy, Catholic, and Apostolic Church to help us answer all the questions we have along the way.

Remember, you are on a journey with God. Along the way you are going to have lots of questions. That's okay. Everyone has questions in their journey with God. A little later we will talk about what to do when you don't know what to do.

When you become a torch set aflame with the love of Christ, wherever you go, whoever you meet, every person and every place that you come in contact with will be set on fire.

Mustard Seeds

My Notes:

_____

_____

_____

_____

_____

_____

_____

2 minutes

tip

Take a moment to ask your students if they have any questions so far. If they do and you don't know the answer, make sure to write the question down and begin the next class by providing the answer. Being willing to say, "I don't know," can have a powerful impact on the children. It shows them that they don't always have to know everything. Continuous learning is an important part of life's journey. If you not only say you don't know the answer, but you actually go back and look it up, this will let your children know you respect their questions and therefore respect them. It will encourage more questions and create an environment of discovery.

Not all of us can fast, or undertake arduous journeys in God's service, or give generous alms, but we can all love. All it takes is the sincere desire to do so.

St. John Bosco

45

WATCH AND DISCUSS

Step-by-Step

1 Introduce Episode 4 by saying: "This episode is longer than others. As you watch, look out for Hemingway as he tries to eat a plate of cupcakes without permission from Sarah."

2 Watch Episode 4.

Be gentle with yourself, be gentle with others, and never stop striving to be all that God created you to be: the-very-best-version-of-yourself.

Resisting Happiness

Temptation, Sin, and Grace

Even though God is constantly trying to show us the best way to live, we are tempted from time to time to wander away from his path.

What is temptation? Temptation is the desire to do something that is unwise or wrong.

We experience temptation in a hundred ways. Sometimes temptation comes in the form of thoughts.

My Notes:

_____

_____

_____

_____

_____

_____

_____

We might think, "Maybe I should copy my friends homework and then I won't have to do it myself." Sometimes our friends lead us into temptation. One of them might say, "Let's go down to the park without telling our parents." And sometimes we lead other people into temptation by suggesting things that don't help them become the-best-version-of-themselves.

In our hearts we know these things are wrong. When was the last time you were tempted to do something that you knew was wrong?

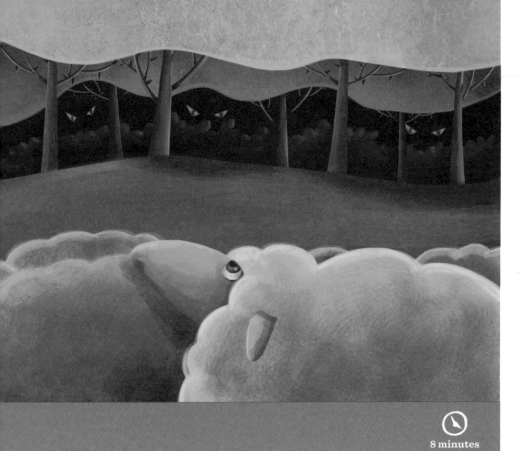

8 minutes

tip

You are about to spend several pages on temptation and sin. It is very easy for the conversation around these topics to become overly negative. Don't let the children lose sight of the whole journey. We all sin from time to time but that is only a piece of the puzzle. The larger context is that you, the pastor, their family, the Church, and God are all here to help them live their best lives. If you need to, don't be afraid to remind the children of that larger context.

Have patience with all things, but chiefly have patience with yourself. Do not lose courage in considering your own imperfections but instantly set about redeeming them— every day begin anew.

St. Francis de Sales

READ AND EXPLORE

Step-by-Step

1 Ask a volunteer to read aloud the prayer about temptation.

2 Ask: "When is a great time to pray?"

- BEFORE MEALS
- BEFORE GOING TO BED
- AT CHURCH ON SUNDAY
- BEFORE AN ACTIVITY, TEST, OR COMPETITION
- IN MOMENTS OF DECISION
- IN MOMENTS OF TEMPTATION

Place prayer at the center of your life and amazing things will begin to happen.

Decision Point

48

Overcoming Temptation

The best way to deal with temptation is to turn to God in prayer and ask him for his help.

Prayer is a conversation with God. Prayer isn't just something we do before meals, or at church on Sunday, or before we go to bed at night. These are all important ways to pray, but God wants you to talk to him throughout the day. At any moment of the day, if you have to make a decision, that's a great time to turn to God in prayer. Ask him to guide you to make the best decision.

My Notes:

_____

_____

_____

_____

_____

_____

_____

_____

God always wants to help you make the right decision. He has given you free will so that you can say yes or no to things, but he wants to help you use your free will to make good and wise decisions. Above all, God has given you free will so that you can love.

Some decisions you make help you become the-best-version-of-yourself, and some do not. Some decisions you make help other people become the-best-version-of-themselves, and some do not. God wants you to always choose the-very-best-version-of-yourself, and to help others become all he created them to be too.

Let's look together at an example.

You are taking a test and you don't know the answer to a question. You may be tempted to cheat by looking at someone else's answer. But cheating won't help you become the-best-version-of-yourself.

Let's pray together right now about temptation.

> Lord, anytime I feel tempted
> to do something that is wrong
> and doesn't help me become
> the-best-version-of-myself,
> please inspire me to choose
> what is good and right.
>
> Amen.

2 minutes

tip

Why is a section about prayer placed within a discussion surrounding temptation, sin, and grace? The answer is simple: The Christian life is not sustainable without prayer. Take a moment and think back to your own life. How much heartache and suffering could you have avoided if you had consulted God in moments of decision and temptation?

You have a great opportunity before you. Most people grow up believing that the only time a person can pray is before a meal, before bed at night, or at church on Sunday. This is a tragedy! You can change that for your children. Encourage them to pray not only every day, but throughout the day, and you will give them a gift of incalculable value.

Nothing is equal to prayer; for what is impossible it makes possible . . .

St. John Chrysostom

READ AND EXPLORE

Step-by-Step

1 Have the children explore the illustration. The artwork depicts the scene in the Gospels in which Jesus is arrested in the Garden of Gethsemane.

2 Take a stretching break. Children this age have a tendency to get restless, and when they get restless they lose focus. Have them stand up, stretch out their legs, and shake off the restlessness.

There is a gentle voice within each of us. What we must do above all else is to learn once again to listen to that gentle voice within us. Only then will we have the peace that we all seek.

The Rhythm of Life

What Is Sin?

God has a marvelous plan for you and your life. As a loving Father, he wants you to become the-best-version-of-yourself by living a holy life.

Sometimes when you are thinking about making a choice that you know you should not make, you get this gnawing, yucky feeling in the pit of your stomach. That feeling is the-best-version-of-yourself, or your conscience, saying, "No, no, no! Don't do it! This is not a good choice for you!"

Sometimes you listen to that voice, and you stop and make a better choice. But at other times, you might continue on and make the bad choice anyway. What happens to that yucky feeling in your belly? It just gets worse because . . . you've sinned against God!

When you have purposely made a poor choice, you have sinned. When you sin you break God's commandments by choosing an action that turns away from him. Some sins hurt our relationship with God; these are called venial sins. Other sins break our relationship with God; these are called mortal sins.

My Notes:

_____

_____

_____

_____

_____

_____

_____

3 minutes

tip

If you are following the suggested 90-minute format, this marks the approximate halfway point. It is a good time for a brief break. If you are running behind, take a quick look ahead and see where you can get back on track. If ahead of schedule, look for an opportunity in the next 45 minutes to spark a great conversation. If on time, press on and finish strong!

The saints did not all begin well, but they all ended well.

St. John Vianney

Step-by-Step

1 Choose a different child to read each of the paragraphs out loud.

> Once found, forgiveness frees. It liberates you from feverishly keeping score and remembering wrongs. It propels you into a new, higher way of living. A life of grace. A life of second chances.

Everybody Needs
To Forgive Somebody

God's Grace

But not everything that makes us feel embarrassed or ashamed is a sin. Mistakes and accidents can make us feel this way too. Let's have a look at an example together.

Perhaps you knock over your milk at breakfast. This is an accident, not a sin. Or maybe you trip over your little sister's toy and break it. This is an accident, not a sin. Maybe you get the answers wrong on your math test or spelling test. This is a mistake, not a sin.

My Notes:

_____
_____
_____
_____
_____
_____
_____

Accidents and mistakes happen. What God wants is for us to avoid intentional sin by making great choices and keeping his commandments.

The best way to deal with sin is to go to Reconciliation. When your body gets sick, you go to the doctor and he or she helps you get better. When your soul gets sick because of sin, you go to Reconciliation and the priest helps you get better.

Through Reconciliation God forgives our sins, but he also gives us grace to help us avoid sin in the future.

What is grace? Grace is the help God gives us to do what is good and right.

God's grace helps us to become the-best-version-of-ourselves. God's grace helps us to grow in virtue. God's grace helps us to live holy lives. God's grace helps us to have healthy relationships. God's grace allows us to share in his life and love.

5 minutes

tip

Often the differences between accidents, mistakes, and sin can cause confusion. Encourage your students to ask questions and explore the differences between accidents and sin, but don't lose sight of the main point: God's grace helps us to avoid sin and do what is good and right.

Grace is not a strange, magic substance which is subtly filtered into our souls to act as a kind of spiritual penicillin. Grace is unity, oneness within ourselves, oneness with God.

Thomas Merton

53

WATCH AND DISCUSS

Step-by-Step

1 Introduce Episode 5 by saying: "In this next episode, Ben enters the biblical world to learn about how Adam and Eve dealt with temptation."

2 Watch Episode 5.

The only way to say no to anything is to have a deeper yes.

The Rhythm of Life

From the Bible: Adam and Eve

Sometimes we use our free will in ways that are good, and sometimes we use it in ways that hurt ourselves and others. This is something the first human beings discovered. Who were the first human beings?

Adam and Eve.

God loved Adam and Eve so much that he blessed them with free will. He gave them a beautiful world to live in and they had everything they needed.

My Notes:

_____

_____

_____

_____

_____

_____

_____

Because he loved them so much, he warned them, "Do not eat the fruit of the tree in the middle of the garden because, if you do, you will die!"

It's important to understand that the reason God didn't want them to eat the fruit was because he loved them so much and didn't want them to hurt themselves.

One day Adam and Eve were in the middle of the garden, near the forbidden tree with the forbidden fruit.

3 minutes

tip

Engaging in self-reflection always leads to improvement. After you try something, ask yourself, "What worked about this? Why? What could I do differently?" Don't worry, if something doesn't initially work out the way you planned. Learning by doing is very effective, and when you reflect, you allow yourself the opportunity to improve.

For Jesus, there are no countries to be conquered, no ideologies to be imposed, no people to be dominated. There are only children, women and men to be loved.

Henri Nouwen

READ AND EXPLORE

Step-by-Step

1 Give time for the students to explore the illustration. Ask them thought-provoking questions like, "Why do you think Eve looks so sad?" "What do you think Adam is thinking about in this image?" "Does the snake look like a good guy or a bad guy?"

A snake came along and started talking to them. Then the snake said, "You should eat the fruit."

"Oh, we can't," Eve said.

"Why not?" asked the snake.

"If we eat it we will die!" Eve explained.

"No you won't," said the snake.

At that moment Adam and Eve began to doubt all the good things that God had done for them and told them.

My Notes:

_____

_____

_____

_____

_____

_____

_____

Forgiveness is at the center of God's heart, it is at the center of this story, and it is central to Christianity.

Rediscover Jesus

Then Eve took the fruit and ate it. She gave some to Adam and he ate it too.

All at once they realized they had made a terrible mistake, and it made them sad. This is the story of original sin and temptation. Original means "first" (Adapted from Genesis 3:1–7).

Adam and Eve experienced temptation and sin, and so do you and I. They made a bad decision. God wants to teach you how to be a great decision maker so you can live a rich, full, happy life in this world—and live with him in heaven in eternal bliss forever.

2 minutes

_____
_____
_____
_____
_____
_____
_____

tip

Our God is a God of surprises. God wants to give you gifts that you haven't even imagined yet. He wants to give you gifts that you can't ask for because you don't know how important they are and you don't know how much you need them, but your God, the ultimate Father, wants to give you these gifts. And the Bible is one of those gifts. The Bible is new every time we read it, not because it changes but because we change. Allow the Bible to become a great companion in your life and in the lives of the children.

Every happening, great and small, is a parable whereby God speaks to us, and the art of life is to get the message.

Malcolm Muggeridge

WATCH AND DISCUSS

Step-by-Step

 1 Introduce Episode 6 by asking: "Can you think of a time when you had that yucky feeling inside you? What was your conscience trying to tell you?"

2 Watch Episode 6.

Everything makes sense in relation to God's dream. When we feel like life is not making sense, it is usually because we have lost sight of God's vision for our lives.

Decision Point

58

Follow Your Conscience

We have been exploring some of the many ways God has blessed you. Life is the greatest blessing. Free will is another fabulous blessing. Both come with great responsibility.

To help you become the-best-version-of-yourself and live a holy life, God has also blessed you with a conscience. Conscience is the gentle voice inside you that encourages you to do good and avoid evil. God speaks to us through our conscience. Your conscience encourages you to become the-best-version-of-yourself. It also warns you when you are thinking of doing something that will offend God and make you unhappy.

My Notes:

_____

_____

_____

_____

_____

_____

_____

_____

The more we listen to our conscience and obey what it tells us, the easier it becomes to hear it. At first it may be difficult to follow our conscience. Lots of things are difficult at first. But don't give up. Keep trying. Never stop trying. God will never give up on you, and you should never give up on yourself.

Following our conscience makes us happy. Ignoring our conscience makes us restless and unhappy.

Do you know what a regret is? A regret is something you wish you had not done. All our regrets come from ignoring our conscience.

Sometimes you are thinking of doing something, but you get a yucky feeling inside or you hear a little voice inside you advising you not to do it. That is your conscience. If you do that thing and ignore your conscience, that yucky feeling will sink deep down into your heart and soul. But if you listen to that gentle voice inside you and do the right thing, you will be glad you did and filled with joy.

Follow your conscience. You will never regret it.

7 minutes

tip
Why is understanding what our conscience is and the role it plays in our lives so important? Well, the whole drama of a person's life can be understood by examining the tension between the--person-I-am and the-person--I-ought-to-be. When we forget that God wants us to live holy lives, we become disoriented. When we lose sight of the great spiritual North Star, we become lost and confused. Everything should be weighed with the journey in mind and the goal in sight. Thus, the question that should be a consistent part of these children's lives is: "Will what I am about to do help me to become the-best--version-of-myself?"

Do not wish to be anything but what you are, and try to be that perfectly.

St. Francis de Sales

Step-by-Step

1 Have four volunteers read the four tips to making a great decision.

2 Share a story of a time when you had to make a really difficult decision and you weren't sure what to do. Did you make the right decision? Did you utilize any of the four steps? If so, how did that help?

When You Don't Know What to Do

There will be times in our lives when we are not sure what to do. When you are faced with a decision and you are unsure what to do, here are some tips to help you make a great decision.

1. Find a quiet place and spend a few minutes listening to your conscience. Ask yourself: What is my conscience encouraging me to do?

2. Think about the Ten Commandments. Ask yourself: Do the Ten Commandments help me see clearly what I should do in this situation?

3. Ask your parents, priest, catechist, or teacher for advice.

4. Pray to the Holy Spirit and ask him to help you make the best decision.

Ask the Holy Spirit to guide you and counsel you—and you will find yourself making better choices.

Decision Point

My Notes:

Nobody is perfect. There will be times when you turn your back on God and his way of doing things. There will be times when you abandon the-best-version-of-yourself. There will be times when you live a selfish life rather than a holy life.

When that happens, recognize it. Don't get discouraged. Go to Reconciliation and start over again. Our God is a God of second chances. Praise be to God! We all need another chance every now and then, and God is always willing to give us another chance and a fresh start. That's just one of the many good reasons why God gives us the incredible gift of Reconciliation.

5 minutes

> I plead with you—
> never, ever give up
> on hope, never doubt,
> never tire, and never
> become discouraged.
> Be not afraid.

St. John Paul II

Step-by-Step

1 Have your children complete the activity page by themselves, with a partner, or as a group.

2 After three minutes ask the class: "Are there any questions you are struggling with?"

3 Briefly explain the answer to any questions they might have referring, back to the specific page in the workbook.

Catholics have been making incredible contributions to the world for 2,000 years. What will your contribution be?

Decision Point

Show What You Know

True or False

1. __T__ We are always happier when we walk in God's ways. (p 40)

2. __F__ If we love God with all our hearts, souls, and minds we won't listen to him. (p 44)

3. __F__ One of the most powerful ways we show God we love him is by being mean to other people. (p 44)

4. __T__ God is constantly trying to show us the best way to live. (p 44)

5. __T__ God has a marvelous plan for you and your life. (p 50)

Fill in the blank

1. God wants you to become a great __decision maker__. (p 57)

2. One of the greatest blessings God has given you is the ability to make __choices__. (p 32)

3. God loves you so much that he blesses you with __free will__. (p 54)

4. The best way to deal with sin is to go to __Reconciliation__. (p 48)

5. By guiding us to make great decisions, God's laws are designed to help us live __happy__ and __holy__ lives. (p 35)

My Notes:

_____

_____

_____

_____

_____

_____

_____

6. The path to happiness begins with saying ____**yes**____ with God and ____**no**____ with God. (p 33)

7. The best way to deal with temptation is to turn to God in ____**prayer**____ and ask him for his help. (p 49)

8. Following our conscience makes us ____**happy**____ and ignoring our conscience makes us restless and ____**unhappy**____. (p 59)

9. God's ____**grace**____ helps us to become the-best-version-of-ourselves. (p 53)

10. Our God is a God of ____**second**____ chances. (p 61)

Word Bank

PRAYER	HOLY
HAPPY	FREE WILL
YES	NO
GRACE	RECONCILIATION
DECISION MAKER	CHOICES
SECOND	UNHAPPY
HAPPY	

10 minutes

tip

If you are running short on time, you may choose to complete this section together as a class. Simply read each fill-in-the-blank and true-or--false statement and invite your students to call out the answer. Once someone calls out the right answer, ask everyone to write it down in their workbook. If you are completely out of time, ask the children to complete the exercise for homework.

Joy is a net of love by which we catch souls.

St. Teresa of Calcutta

JOURNAL WITH JESUS

Step-by-Step

1. Invite your children to write a letter to Jesus.

2. Ask the children to remain silent during their journaling time.

3. You may wish to play some quiet, reflective music to help create the right mood in the classroom and to encourage the students to remain quiet and focused on journaling with Jesus.

You have a unique blend of talents and abilities that are perfectly suited to carry out whatever mission God has assigned to you on this earth.

Decision Point

My Notes:

_____

_____

_____

_____

_____

_____

_____

_____

Journal with Jesus

Dear Jesus,

I am the-best-version-of-myself when I . . .

_____

_____

_____

_____

_____

_____

_____

🕐 **5 minutes**

_____

_____

_____

_____

_____

_____

Remember you have only one soul; that you have only one death to die; that you have only one life, which is short and has to be lived by you alone; and there is one glory, which is eternal. If you do this there will be a great many things about which you care nothing.

St. Theresa of Ávila

CLOSING PRAYER

Step-by-Step

1 Introduce Episode 7 by saying: "It's time for the closing prayer; let's quiet down and get ready to pray with Ben."

2 Watch Episode 7.

3 Ask your children: "What are some of the most important things you learned in this session?"

- I AM ALWAYS HAPPIER WHEN I WALK WITH GOD.
- GOD WILL NEVER GIVE UP ON ME!
- GOD WANTS ME TO BE A GREAT DECISION MAKER.

God works in powerful ways through his Commandments.

Decision Point

Closing Prayer

Throughout the Bible we read about angels helping people. There are three Archangels whom God has given great power to. Their names are Michael, Gabriel, and Raphael. The Church also teaches that God has appointed an angel for every person—including you. We call this angel your Guardian Angel.

Your Guardian Angel is there to guide and protect you. The Church invites us to pray this special prayer to our Guardian Angel:

> **Angel of God,**
> **my Guardian dear,**
> **to whom God's love commits me here,**
> **ever this day be at my side,**
> **to light and guard, to rule and guide.**
>
> **Amen.**

This is a great prayer to begin the day with. It also is a great prayer to pray when we are afraid. You may even want to name your Guardian Angel, so you can speak with him or her throughout the day.

My Notes:

_____

_____

_____

_____

_____

_____

_____

3 minutes

Be who you are and be that well.

St. Francis de Sales

3

God Sent Jesus to Save Us

QUICK SESSION OVERVIEW

Opening Prayer. . . . . 2 min

Watch and Discuss; Read and Explore . . . . 68 min

Show What You Know . . . . 10 min

Journal with Jesus . . . . 5 min

Closing Prayer. . . . . 5 min

OBJECTIVES

- **TO DEMONSTRATE** that our story and Jesus' story are connected.

- **TO EXPLAIN** that God will go to unimaginable lengths to prove his love to us.

- **TO TEACH** that Jesus invites us to have a dynamic and personal relationship with him so that he can share his happiness with us and we can share it with others.

• Greet the children at the door.

• Let them know you are excited for them to discover Jesus.

1 WELCOME

If there is one person we should each get to know in a deeply personal way, it is Jesus.

That's precisely why the task before you is so important! There is no story, no person more important for these young people to discover than Jesus. And, believe it or not, this might be the one opportunity these young people have to encounter Jesus in a powerful way.

It's good for you to take some time to feel the weight of this great task. It will give you a sense of urgency and a higher level of focus. But be careful not to let it overwhelm you. The temptation to think, "That's too great a task; I am only one person, after all!" will be tremendous.

When that thought enters your mind, take a step back and look at what other great men and women before you have done in the span of just one lifetime: Francis of Assisi, St. Paul, Thomas Aquinas, John the Baptist, St. Augustine, Teresa of Ávila, Thomas More, Joan of Arc, Edmund Rice, Don Bosco, John Vianney, Dominic, Patrick, Rita, Mary, and of course Jesus. Look also at what others have done in our time: St. Teresa of Calcutta and St. John Paul II.

They too could have used the excuse, "I am only one person." The difference is, they didn't see themselves as one person, but rather as part of one body. Then, dedicated to the Gospel message of Jesus Christ, they chose to serve, and choosing to serve is choosing to love.

Remember, Blessed is the fruit of thousands of hours of research, development, and testing. Every word, every image, every activity has been scrutinized, evaluated, and prayed over. You are not alone.

Prayer Icon

Read and Explore

Watch and Discuss

Show What You Know

Journal with Jesus

Time Tracker

OPENING PRAYER

Step-by-Step

1 Gather students for prayer. Wait for them to be quiet. Don't rush this; reverence takes patience and practice. Before reading the prayer aloud, take a deep breath to allow an additional moment of silence. You never know what God might say to your students (or you!) when given the opportunity.

Every yearning you have for good things is in some way a yearning for God.

Decision Point

My Notes:

3
God Sent Jesus to Save Us

God, our loving Father,
thank you for all the ways you bless me.
Help me to be aware that every person,
place, and adventure I experience is an
opportunity to love you more.
Fill me with a desire to change and to grow,
and give me the wisdom to choose
the-best-version-of-myself in
every moment of every day.

Amen.

2 minutes

tip
Being specific lets your students know what is needed. A firm, not angry, voice sets the tone. "We are not talking right now; we are praying." "I am waiting on everyone to close their eyes to begin."

The earnest prayer of a righteous person has great power and wonderful results.

James 5:16

69

WATCH AND DISCUSS

Step-by-Step

1 Introduce Episode 1 by saying: "In this episode Sarah saves Hemingway from a messy situation with some ice cream. Have you ever needed to be saved from a mess?"

2 Watch Episode 1.

3 Ask: "Jesus is Savior of the world. What does that mean?"

- BEING SAVIOR OF THE WORLD MEANS THAT JESUS SAVED EVERY PERSON WHO HAS EVER LIVED, AND WHO WILL EVER LIVE, FROM OUR SINS SO THAT WE CAN BE HAPPY ON EARTH AND HAPPY WITH GOD IN HEAVEN.

- IF THEY NEED HELP FINDING THE ANSWER, POINT THEM TO THE TEXT IN THE WORKBOOK.

My Notes:

_____

_____

_____

_____

_____

_____

_____

The Mess

Since the beginning, human beings have been trying to figure out the best way to live. God often sent great prophets to lead and guide the people, but many of the people didn't listen to them. Finally, when the time was just right, God sent his only Son, Jesus.

The world was a mess because people were confused about who they were and the purpose of life. They were lost. They needed to be saved from their selfishness and sin.

So God sent his Son, Jesus, to save them. And he didn't send Jesus just for the people of that time; he sent Jesus to save the people of all times. Do you need to be saved from your selfishness?

You see, your story and Jesus' story are connected. Jesus' story is not just about what happened two thousand years ago. It is also about your friendship with him today.

We all need to be saved, and people who need to be saved need a savior. Jesus is the Savior of the world. What does that mean?

10 minutes

_____
_____
_____
_____
_____
_____
_____

For God so loved the world that he gave his only son, so that everyone who believes in him will not perish but have eternal life.

John 3:16

Step-by-Step

1 Give the children a moment
or two to explore the
illustration. And yes, that
is a shark fin in the water!

2 If you have a story of a
time when you were saved,
share that story with
the children.

**Embrace the life
and teachings of
Jesus like you would
a good friend whom
you have not seen
for a long time.**

Decision Point

We All Need Saving

Imagine you went into a store and ate an ice cream, even though you
didn't have the money to pay for it. This would be wrong and illegal,
and the storeowner would have every right to be very angry with
you and call the police. But just at that moment a friend of yours
comes into the store, realizes what is happening, and gives his own
money to the store owner to pay for the ice cream you stole. Your
friend has paid your debt. In this situation, your friend has saved you.

Another example would be if you went swimming at the beach and
got caught in the current and carried out to sea. As the waves get
bigger and you become tired, you start drowning.

But just at that moment a lifeguard comes along in a rescue boat
and brings you safely back to shore. The lifeguard has saved you.

My Notes:

_____

_____

_____

_____

_____

_____

_____

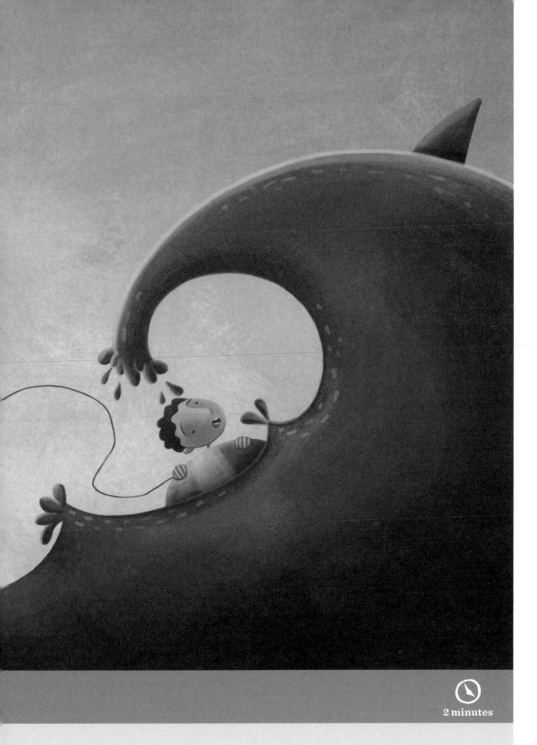

2 minutes

Keep your sense of humor close by. Teaching the Catholic faith is a serious task; there's probably nothing more important. But it's also supposed to be fun. You never want to lose sight of the joy of being with young children. When a child does something humorous, share in his or her delight. It's easy to obsess over problems and worry about things you wish you'd done differently. Humor, though, brings much needed perspective. If you can maintain your humor, you'll be a much happier leader—and most likely, a better one, too.

The Lord himself goes before you and will be with you; he will never leave you nor forsake you. Do not be afraid; do not be discouraged.

Deuteronomy 31:8

Step-by-Step

1 Remind your students: "When Jesus was on the cross, he thought of you!"

2 Ask them: "How does this make you feel?" Possible answers include the following:

- GRATEFUL
- HAPPY
- BLESSED

Jesus teaches that the essence of love is self-donation.

Decision Point

Jesus is Your Savior

Now, think about all the men, women, and children since the beginning of time, and the many things that they have done that are selfish and wrong and offend God. Jesus came and paid the price for all of these sins by dying for you and me on the cross. Why? Because he wants you to be happy with him forever in heaven. Amazing, isn't it? When Jesus was on the cross, he thought of you. He loved you then and he loves you now.

Many people can save you from various situations, but only Jesus can save you from your sins.

My Notes:

_____

_____

_____

_____

_____

_____

_____

2 minutes

tip

Use repetition and reinforcement to your advantage. You can't expect your students to gain new knowledge after just one exposure. Repetition is key! This may be the first time some of your children learn that Jesus died out of love for them. This is a HUGE deal! Through repetition and reinforcement, you will be letting them know how important this reality is for their lives.

Jesus also suffered for you, leaving you an example, that you should follow in his footsteps.

1 Peter 2:21

WATCH AND DISCUSS

Step-by-Step

1 Introduce Episode 2 by asking: "Are you ready to meet Ben and Sarah's baby sister, Lily?"

2 Watch Episode 2.

3 Activity: SIMON SAYS

To play, perform a quick movement, like touching your nose, stating the movement as you do it. Unless you say, "Simon says," before you describe the movement, the children should not do it. If a child does the action without your saying "Simon Says" first, he or she is out and should sit down. Work fast to make it more difficult and to add humor. The sillier the movement, the more fun the group will have. Play until all the children are sitting or until two minutes have passed.

Jesus' Birth & Childhood

Jesus had a huge mission: to save every sinner in history from their sins. That's a big mission, right?

And yet, God in his wisdom decided not to come as the king of a great nation or as a powerful political leader. He didn't even come as the son of a rich man, but as a baby born in a stable.

What lesson does this teach us? God's ways are not man's ways.

God has a unique way of doing things. He has wisdom far beyond that of the wisest men and women in this world. His ways are far superior to our own ways. He has a better plan for your life than any you could dream up for yourself. Ask God to fill you with his wisdom, so that you can learn his way of doing things.

My Notes:

_____

_____

_____

_____

_____

_____

_____

God came into the world as a tiny, helpless child. Every year we celebrate the miracle of Jesus' birth. Christmas is Jesus' birthday. But if Christmas is Jesus' birthday, why do you get presents?

5 minutes

tip

Listening skills are essential to living a rich and rewarding life. It is impossible to have great relationships if you are not a good listener. But most people are not good listeners. Explain to the students that one of the practical life skills they are developing throughout this program is the ability to really listen to God. Simon Says is a great way to help the children learn the importance of listening in a fun and entertaining way.

> **Whenever man attempts to do what he knows to be the Master's will, a power will be given him equal to the duty.**
>
> Venerable Fulton J. Sheen

READ AND EXPLORE

Step-by-Step

1 Have students think of a time when they lost something important to them. How did they feel when they lost it? Did they find it? If so, how did they feel when they found it? Feel free to participate and share a time when you lost and then found something important to you. Don't forget to thank them for sharing!

2 Give the children an opportunity to explore the illustration. Ask them: "How do you think Mary and Joseph felt when they found Jesus?"

> You can't ignore Jesus, because he changed things. He is the single greatest agent of change in human history.

Rediscover Catholicism

78

The Quiet Years

After Jesus' birth, we know very little about the next thirty years of his life. What do you think he was doing?

Everything would suggest that Jesus lived a very normal life. His daily routines would have been very similar to those of other boys and girls he grew up with.

We do catch a glimpse of Jesus' childhood when he was traveling with Mary and Joseph to Jerusalem. During this trip Jesus got separated from his parents. Eventually they found him in the Temple.

Have you ever lost something important and then found it again? What did it feel like when you realized you had lost it? How did you feel when you found it? How do you think Mary and Joseph felt when they could not find Jesus?

My Notes:

_____

_____

_____

_____

_____

_____

_____

_____

5 minutes

tip

Try to involve everyone in the conversation. Ask the boys and the girls an equal number of questions. Look around the room. Move the conversation around the classroom, trying to involve as much of the class as possible.

We have what we seek, it is there all the time, and if we give it time, it will make itself known to us.

Thomas Merton

79

Step-by-Step

1. Introduce Episode 3 by saying: "I hope you are as excited as I am to learn about the life of Jesus!"

2. Watch Episode 3.

3. Activity: STRETCH! Guide students in some stretching exercises. Have them stand up and follow your directions for an easy, instant energizer.

For more than two thousand years Jesus has been performing miracles in the lives of ordinary men and women. Now he wants to perform miracles in you and through you. Are you ready?

Rediscover Jesus

Jesus' Ministry

The next we hear about Jesus is at the wedding in Cana. They ran out of wine and Mary asked Jesus to help. So Jesus asked the servants to fill six large jars with water and Jesus transformed the water into wine. This was his first miracle.

No doubt word quickly spread about this miracle, which would have made it very difficult for Jesus to return to a normal life. This was the beginning of Jesus' public life, during which he made his way around the region teaching and healing many people.

Jesus was fully divine, but he was also fully human. He loved the everyday aspects of life as a human being. We often see him enjoying a meal with friends and strangers. Here we see him celebrating at a wedding. Jesus loved life.

My Notes:

_____

_____

_____

_____

_____

_____

_____

10 minutes

tip

If you are following the
suggested 90-minute format,
this marks the approximate
halfway point. It is a good time
for a brief break. If you are
running behind, take a quick
look ahead and see where
you can get back on track. If
ahead of schedule, look for
an opportunity in the next
45 minutes to spark a great
conversation. If on time, press
on and finish strong!

_____
_____
_____
_____
_____
_____
_____

**I came that they may
have life and have it
abundantly.**

John 10:10

81

READ AND EXPLORE

Step-by-Step

1. Popcorn! Ask a different student to read each paragraph.

2. Ask the children: "How can you carry on Jesus' mission?" Remind them what Ben told Sarah when she asked him that very question.

   - BEING A GREAT FRIEND
   - TREATING OTHERS HOW I WANT TO BE TREATED
   - FOLLOWING THE COMMANDMENTS
   - GOING TO MASS

> It is easy to be a follower, but to be a disciple means to be a student— to be humble, docile, and teachable, and to listen.
>
> Rediscover Catholicism

The Disciples

One of the things Jesus loved about life was friendship. At the beginning of his ministry, he surrounded himself with twelve disciples. He personally invited each of them to follow him. He knew that he was going to die to bring salvation to all humanity, and that others would be needed to carry on the mission.

In every place and in every time, Jesus calls men, women, and children to follow him and carry on his mission. He invites you to become one of his disciples in the world today.

How can you carry on Jesus' mission?

My Notes:

_____

_____

_____

_____

_____

_____

_____

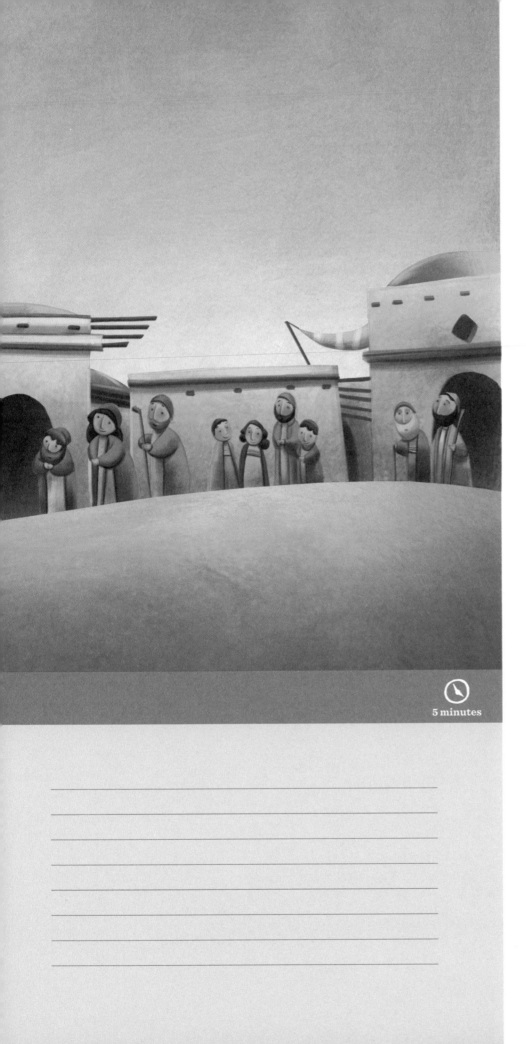

5 minutes

We must be living witnesses of the beauty and grandeur of Christianity.

St. Gianna Molla

READ AND EXPLORE

Step-by-Step

1 Share with the children your favorite parable.

2 Ask the children, which parable is their favorite.

Jesus' Parables

Throughout his public life Jesus used parables to share his wisdom with ordinary people. These parables were easy for ordinary people to understand because they were based on examples from everyday life.

Jesus taught in this way because the religious leaders of his time had made everything very complicated. Jesus wanted ordinary people to be able to understand his message and make their way to God. He taught us that there is genius in simplicity. One of the most difficult things in the world to do is to take something that is complex and make it simple.

Which parable is your favorite?

Jesus was a radical. His life was radical. His death was radical. His teachings were radical. His love was radical. It changed the entire course of human history.

Rediscover Jesus

My Notes:

_____

_____

_____

_____

_____

_____

_____

3 minutes

tip

How into this session are you? Your students can tell. Get into it. If you don't feel like you are into it enough, spend some more time preparing for each session. Preparation breeds confidence.

Christ's teaching will never let us down, while worldly wisdom always will.

St. Vincent de Paul

85

READ AND EXPLORE

Step-by-Step

1 Ask the children: "If you could perform one of Jesus' miracles today, which would you choose? Why?"

It is easy to fall into the trap of placing Jesus' miracles in a far-off place with people you never knew. But they are also here and now. It's a miracle that he forgives our sins even though he knows we will sin again. Would you forgive someone if you knew he or she was going to do it again?

Rediscover Jesus

86

The Miracles of Jesus

Jesus performed hundreds of miracles. He healed the sick, made the blind see and the lame walk, and comforted the afflicted. He didn't do these things to show off or amaze people. Jesus performed miracles because he felt tremendous mercy for people and wanted to demonstrate the awesome compassion he had for those who were struggling and suffering. He also wanted people to be absolutely clear that he was not just a great teacher, but that he was God.

God has great compassion for his people. One of the ways we can share in Jesus' mission is by bringing his compassion to everyone who crosses our path in life.

If you could perform one of Jesus' miracles today, which would you choose? Why?

My Notes:

_____

_____

_____

_____

_____

_____

_____

3 minutes

The most incredible thing about miracles . . . is that they happen.

G.K. Chesterton

WATCH AND DISCUSS

Step-by-Step

1 Give them a preview of the next episode. Tell them why they are going to like it. But make sure you don't give too much away. This also lets them know that you are preparing for your time together. Don't think this is a meaningless act. They notice. And it matters.

2 Watch Episode 4.

Life requires courage. Courage animates us and is therefore essential to the human experience

Decision Point

My Notes:

_____

_____

_____

_____

_____

_____

_____

_____

_____

The Cross, Resurrection, and Ascension

Most people thought it was just another Friday, but it wasn't. We call the day Jesus died on the cross Good Friday because it was the day that Jesus saved us from our sins and repaired our relationship with God. On that day Jesus was beaten, bullied, mocked, spat upon, cursed at, and crucified on the cross. Jesus knew all this would happen, and he let it happen anyway, because he loved us so much that he was willing to lay down his life for us.

God loves you so much. He will go to unimaginable lengths to prove his love for you.

8 minutes

tip

This whole session is about the life of Jesus and how he invites us to be a part of his story. Don't let this be the last time you talk about it though. Don't let up on the Jesus thing. We don't talk anywhere near enough about friendship with Jesus. Keep coming back to it. If we can help them develop this friendship with Jesus, a lot of other things will just fall into place.

The crucifix does not signify defeat or failure. It reveals to us the love that overcomes evil and sin.

Pope Francis

Step-by-Step

1 Ask the children: "Do you want to go to heaven?" We can never spend too much time encouraging and helping our young people to think about heaven and the joy that awaits us.

> **Every moment of every day, every situation, every person we encounter is an opportunity to become a-better-version-of-ourselves.**
>
> Resisting Happiness

The Resurrection

On Sunday morning, three days after Jesus died on the cross, he rose from the dead. We call this the Resurrection. Never before and never since has anyone raised himself from the dead.

The Resurrection is the most important event in history.

One of the reasons that Jesus died on the cross and rose from the dead was so that we could go to heaven. God wants you to live with him and the angels and saints in heaven forever.

Do you want to go to heaven? Why?

My Notes:

_____

_____

_____

_____

_____

_____

_____

The Ascension

For forty days after he rose from the dead, Jesus appeared to many people. Then he took the eleven remaining disciples out to a place near Bethany. He blessed them and then ascended into heaven, forty days after the Resurrection.

We call this the Ascension.

Jesus is a bridge between heaven and earth. By ascending into heaven he cleared the way for us to receive the ultimate blessing: eternal life.

You are blessed.

Why were there only eleven disciples at the Ascension?

2 minutes

tip
Be you. Throughout your time together with these children, make sure they are getting to know you.

> **The goal of our life is to live with God forever. God, who loves us, gave us life, our own response of love allows God's life to flow into us without limit.**
>
> St. Ignatius of Loyola

WATCH AND DISCUSS

Step-by-Step

1 Give the children time and space to explore the illustration. Let them ask questions and let the Holy Spirit inspire their imagination and sense of wonder.

2 Introduce Episode 5 by saying: "I am so excited to share this episode with you because the story of Pentecost is amazing! What you are about to watch really happened."

3 Watch Episode 5.

> Read the Gospels and observe those who live by fear. Look also at those who trust Jesus and live by faith. Don't let fear paralyze you.

Mustard Seeds

From the Bible: Pentecost

Before Jesus left the disciples to ascend into heaven he promised to send the Holy Spirit to help them live good lives and carry out their mission. Jesus makes that same promise to you. He promised to send the Holy Spirit to guide you so you can make great decisions, become the-best-version-of-yourself, live a holy life, and help other people experience God's love.

At Pentecost Jesus kept his promise.

After Jesus died on the cross, rose from the dead, and ascended into heaven, many people were angry at his disciples. The disciples were afraid of what the angry people might do to them.

My Notes:

_____

_____

_____

_____

_____

_____

_____

One day they were all gathered together in an upper room when they heard a loud sound like a howling wind. Then the Holy Spirit descended upon them and filled them with the wisdom and courage they needed to carry out the mission Jesus had entrusted to them.

When you were baptized the Holy Spirit came upon you, and when you get confirmed the gifts of the Holy Spirit will be strengthened in you. This will allow you to continue Jesus' mission in your own way.

Before the Holy Spirit came the disciples were afraid. After they received the Holy Spirit they were filled with courage, and they went out and changed the world. If you are ever afraid, ask the Holy Spirit to fill you with courage.

There are many things that we cannot do on our own, but with God's grace and the power of the Holy Spirit we can do great things.

3 minutes

tip

How is your relationship with the Holy Spirit? The power and grace given to the disciples at Pentecost is available to us now. Sadly many of us spend our entire lives without knowing how powerful the Holy Spirit can be when called upon. At least once a day for the next week, pray to the Holy Spirit and ask him to guide you in a specific question.

Be strong and courageous. Do not be afraid; do not be discouraged, for the Lord your God will be with you wherever you go.

Joshua 1:9

WATCH AND DISCUSS

Step-by-Step

1 Introduce Episode 6 by saying: "In this next episode, Ben, Sarah, and Hemingway prepare for Isabella's surprise birthday party."

2 Watch Episode 6.

The truth is, you cannot become the-best-version-of-yourself on your own. You need grace. The fullness of the invitation is to become the-best-version-of-yourself in Jesus.

Decision Point

You and the Church

Pentecost is the birthday of the Church. We celebrate Pentecost every year, just like you celebrate your birthday.

Jesus gave us the Church to pass his message on to the people of every place and every time. On Sunday at Mass Jesus' message is passed on to you and your family.

My Notes:

_____

_____

_____

_____

_____

_____

The Church also passes along the Sacraments, so that you can continue to receive the grace you need to you need to become the-best-version-of-youself, grow in virtue, and live a holy life.

You are blessed to be a member of the One, Holy, Catholic, and Apostolic Church.

How do you think it would have been different being a Christian two thousand years ago than it is today?

5 minutes

tip

You have probably already discovered that the hardest part of making this a powerful experience is classroom management. You are in charge. Make sure your students know it. You don't need to scream or shout, but you do need to be firm, confident, and prepared.

Courageously follow the path of personal holiness and diligently nourish yourselves with the word of God and the Eucharist. The holier you are, the more you can contribute to building up the Church and society.

St. John Paul II

READ AND EXPLORE

Step-by-Step

1 Ask your students: "If you could be anyone in the Jesus story, who would you be?" If they need help, make suggestions: one of the disciples, Mary, Lazarus, Zacchaeus, the woman at the well, the Good Shepherd, etc.

When we remove ourselves from the story of Jesus Christ, we become immune to the life-changing message of the Gospel and become slaves to the world.

Rediscover Jesus

You

Jesus' story doesn't stop there. In fact, for you Jesus' story is just beginning. He wants you to be part of his story.

It's real. Just like the lepers, the prodigal son, the woman at the well, and the disciples, Jesus wants you to be part of his story. And he wants to be part of your story too.

If you could be any person in the Jesus story, who would you be?

The Jesus story never ends. It is unfolding here, today, right now. And Jesus wants you to be a part of the story.

My Notes:

_____

_____

_____

_____

_____

_____

_____

_____

You are blessed to be part of the story. The mess of the world can make us sad at times, but Jesus wants us to be supremely happy. He invites us to have a dynamic and personal relationship with him so that he can share his happiness with us and we can share it with others.

So, each morning when you wake up and each night before you go to bed, take a minute to talk to Jesus.

tip

Take a moment to tell them why you love being a part of Jesus' story.

5 minutes

What really matters in life is that we are loved by Christ and that we love him in return. In comparison to the love of Jesus, everything is secondary. And, without the love of Jesus, everything else is useless.

St. John Paul II

97

Step-by-Step

1 Have your children complete the activity page by themselves, with a partner, or as a group.

2 After three minutes ask the class: "Are there any questions you are struggling with?"

3 Briefly explain the answer to any questions they might have, referring back to the specific page in the workbook.

Courage is a prerequisite for the life God has envisioned for you.

Decision Point

98

Show What You Know

True or False

1. __T__ When Jesus was on the cross, he thought of you because he loves you. (p 74)

2. __T__ Jesus wants you to become one of his disciples. (p 82)

3. __T__ You are blessed to be a member of the Catholic Church. (p 95)

4. __F__ The Sacraments help make you the-worst-version-of-yourself. (p 95)

5. __T__ Jesus wants you to be a part of his story. (p 96)

Fill in the blank

1. Jesus ____loves____ life. (p 80)

2. It takes ____wisdom____ to be able to see God's ways and walk in them. (p 76)

3. Jesus wanted ____ordinary____ people to be able to understand his message and make their way to God. (p 84)

4. God will go to unimaginable lengths to prove his ____love____ for you. (p 89)

5. Jesus performed miracles because he felt tremendous ____mercy____ for people. (p 86)

My Notes:

_____

_____

_____

_____

_____

_____

_____

_____

6. The __Resurrection__ is the most important event in history. (p 90)

7. God wants you to live with him and the angels and saints in __heaven__ forever. (p 90)

8. Jesus is a __bridge__ between heaven and earth. (p 91)

9. With God's grace and the power of the __Holy__ __Spirit__ we can do great things. (p 93)

10. Jesus invites you to have a __dynamic__ and __personal__ relationship with him so that he can share his happiness with us and we can share it with others. (p 97)

Word Bank

LOVE	DYNAMIC	HOLY SPIRIT	WISDOM	HEAVEN	MERCY
LOVES	PERSONAL	ORDINARY	BRIDGE	RESURRECTION	

🕐 **10 minutes**

_____

_____

_____

_____

_____

_____

_____

tip

Let students know that making mistakes is all right. Children often fear making a mistake or being embarrassed by not knowing an answer. Here are some tips for letting children know it's all right to make an error:

- WHEN YOU MAKE A MISTAKE, CALL ATTENTION TO IT IN A LIGHTHEARTED WAY

- LET THEM KNOW YOU DON'T HAVE ALL THE ANSWERS

- TURN INCORRECT ANSWERS INTO POSITIVE TEACHING MOMENTS BY SAYING THINGS LIKE:

In some situations, that might work, but…

That is a good answer, but I think there is one that works better for that sentence.

I thought so too until I reread page X and learned…

Thank you for your answer. Did anyone else have a different answer?

God resists the proud, but gives grace to the humble.

James 4:6

JOURNAL WITH JESUS

Step-by-Step

1. Invite your children to write a letter to Jesus.

2. Ask the children to remain silent during their journaling time.

3. You may wish to play some quiet, reflective music to help create the right mood in the classroom and to encourage the students to remain quiet and focused on journaling with Jesus.

One of the ways God loves us is by revealing himself to us. He does not remain a distant, anonymous God; he allows us to know him.

Decision Point

My Notes:

_____

_____

_____

_____

_____

_____

_____

Journal with Jesus

Dear Jesus,

Learning about your life teaches me . . .

_____

_____

_____

_____

_____

_____

_____

🕐 **5 minutes**

_____

_____

_____

_____

_____

_____

Few souls understand what God would accomplish in them if they were to abandon themselves unreservedly to him and if they were to allow his grace to mold them accordingly.

St. Ignatius of Loyola

CLOSING PRAYER

Step-by-Step

1 Watch Episode 7.

2 Ask the children: "What are some of the most important things you learned in this session?"

- I AM A PART OF JESUS' STORY!
- JESUS HAS A SPECIAL MISSION JUST FOR ME.
- GOD LOVES ME ENOUGH TO GIVE HIS LIFE FOR ME.
- JESUS WANTS ME TO SHARE HIS LOVE WITH OTHERS.

To pray is to talk to God about anything that is in your heart: the things that bring you joy and the things that bring you sorrow; your hopes and dreams. In prayer you talk to God about everything.

Decision Point

Closing Prayer

Jesus said, "Ask and you shall receive" (Matthew 7:7). There are going to be times in your life when you don't know what to do. That's a great time to turn to the Holy Spirit and ask for insight. There are going to be times in your life when you need encouragement. The Holy Spirit is the great encourager. Turn to him and ask him to encourage you. There are going to be times in your life when you are afraid. Ask the Holy Spirit to give you courage. There are going to be times in your life when you don't know what to say. Turn to the Holy Spirit and ask him to give you the words.

We all have a daily need for the Holy Spirit. As we grow older we become less dependent on some people and some things, but we always need the Holy Spirit's guidance.

Saint Augustine wandered far away from God when he was young, but then he went to Reconciliation, turned back to God, and ultimately became a great priest and bishop.

Let's pray his prayer to the Holy Spirit together:

Breathe into me, Holy Spirit, that my thoughts may all be holy. Move in me, Holy Spirit, that my work, too, may be holy. Attract my heart, Holy Spirit, that I may love only what is holy. Strengthen me, Holy Spirit, that I may defend all that is holy. Protect me, Holy Spirit, that I may always be holy.

Amen.

My Notes:

_____

_____

_____

_____

_____

_____

5 minutes

tip

Tell them something you learned from this session that you didn't know before.

By turning your eyes on God in meditation, your whole soul will be filled with God. Begin all your prayers in the presence of God.

St. Francis de Sales

103

4

Forgiveness and Healing

QUICK SESSION OVERVIEW

Opening Prayer. . . . . 2 min

Watch and Discuss; Read and Explore . . . . 68 min

Show What You Know . . . . 10 min

Journal with Jesus . . . . 5 min

Closing Prayer. . . . . 5 min

OBJECTIVES

- **TO DEMONSTRATE** that forgiveness is key to healthy relationships.

- **TO EXPLAIN** that Jesus, the Good Shepherd, leads us to heaven.

- **TO TEACH** that, in the Sacrament of Reconciliation God proves that he is always willing to forgive us.

- ## Start on time anyway.

- ## Systems drive behavior—if you want them to be on time, you need to start on time.

1 WELCOME

As you start class, begin by thanking your children for coming. Remind them you will be praying for them during the week. Remember, if you cannot convince them that you care about them, you will not be able to deliver a life-changing experience.

Then, remind them of one of the key points from the previous session (just like TV shows start with "Previously on . . . " followed by a short highlight reel from the recent episode).

Ask them what they remember about the life of Jesus. What stuck out to them? Was it his miracles or teachings? Was it the Resurrection or Ascension? Was it the story of Pentecost?

When the children share what they remember, go out of your way to affirm them. Give them a high-five or a token of congratulations like a sticker or piece of candy. Help them to feel special for remembering and having the courage to speak up.

Prayer Icon

Read and Explore

Watch and Discuss

Show What You Know

Journal with Jesus

Time Tracker

OPENING PRAYER

Step-by-Step

1 Pray the opening prayer.

2 Allow them a moment of quiet before you start reading the prayer. You could say something like, "Let's just take a moment in silence to be still and quiet and open ourselves up to whatever God wants to tell us today."

If you want to see something incredible, start by praying for transformation.

Decision Point

My Notes:

_____

_____

_____

_____

_____

_____

_____

4

Forgiveness and Healing

God, our loving Father,
thank you for all the ways you bless me.
Help me to be aware that every person,
place, and adventure I experience is an
opportunity to love you more.
Fill me with a desire to change and to grow,
and give me the wisdom to choose
the-best-version-of-myself in
every moment of every day.

Amen.

2 minutes

tip

Have the children begin with the Sign of the Cross, and invite them to close their eyes as you read the opening prayer slowly and deliberately. Then give them thirty seconds in silence to reflect on the prayer and what God is saying to them through it.

If you wish to go to extremes, let it be in sweetness, patience, humility, and charity.

St. Philip Neri

WATCH AND DISCUSS

Step-by-Step

1 Introduce Episode 1: "In this episode, Sarah and Hemingway have a surprise for Ben. What do you think it could be?"

2 Watch Episode 1.

The wiser you become, the closer you will want to be to God

Decision Point

106

God Loves Healthy Relationships

God loves relationships. He delights in his relationship with you, and he delights in your healthy relationships with others.

God is a perfect friend because he always helps you become the-best-version-of-yourself. Other people might ask you to do things that will lead you to become a-second-rate-version-of-yourself, but not God. Everything he asks you to do comes from his desire for you to become the-best-version-of-yourself, live a holy life, and be happy.

My Notes:

Forgiveness is essential to healthy relationships. Two of the most important life lessons are how to forgive and how to be forgiven. These two lessons are part of the Our Father prayer. We pray, "Forgive us our trespasses as we forgive those who trespass against us." We are saying sorry to God for any wrong we have done and asking him to give us the grace to forgive anyone who has wronged us.

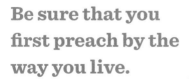

5 minutes

tip
How many students are in your class? How many of them believe that you want what is best for them? Have you convinced them that you have their best interests at heart? We respect and listen to people we believe have our best interests at heart. If you have not won them in this way yet, ask yourself why.

Be sure that you first preach by the way you live.

St. Charles Borromeo

107

WATCH AND DISCUSS

Step-by-Step

 1 Introduce Episode 2: "Whose toothbrush do you think Sarah accidentally uses to brush Hemingway's hair? Let's find out!"

2 Watch Episode 2.

3 Have the students share with a partner the last time they forgave someone. If they are struggling, remind them of when Ben destroyed Sarah's painting with a football and how Sarah carelessly used Ben's toothbrush to comb Hemingway's hair.

When we choose not to forgive, we turn our backs on God and the-best-version-of-ourselves.

Rediscover Jesus

Forgiveness

Have you ever done something that you knew was wrong? How did it make you feel?

We all mess up and make bad choices sometimes. Saint Paul teaches us that we have all sinned and fallen short of God's dreams for us. These are just some of the reasons that God blesses us with the Sacrament of Reconciliation.

My Notes:

_____

_____

_____

_____

_____

_____

_____

When was the last time you forgave someone? When was the last time someone forgave you?

We don't talk about forgiveness to blame ourselves or to feel bad about ourselves. God doesn't want that. We talk about these things so we can do something about them.

10 minutes

tip

When you are advising or helping your students, try not to tell them the negative things they shouldn't do; instead, tell them the positive things they should do.

Be kind and compassionate to one another, forgiving each other, just as Christ God forgave you.

Ephesians 4:32

Step-by-Step

1 Read the text aloud. If it works for your class, you can read the action while one student reads Max's lines and another reads Max's mom's lines.

You cannot become more like Christ and stay as you are.

Mustard Seeds

Max and His Room

Here's a story to help us all understand. One day Max got his very own bedroom. Everything was perfect and in its place. But the next day, after church, Max threw his nice church clothes on the floor as he got changed to go outside and play with his friends. He didn't realize it at the time, but this was the beginning of a growing problem.

The next day Max threw his pajamas on the floor instead of putting them where they belong. That afternoon after soccer he left his soccer gear on the floor in the middle of the room. The following day he had some potato chips and a candy bar, but instead of putting the wrappers in the trash can, he threw them on the floor.

This went on for three weeks. Max just kept throwing things where they didn't belong.

My Notes:

_____

_____

_____

_____

_____

_____

_____

Then one day he came home and he couldn't open the door to his room. He went looking for his mother and asked, "Mom, why did you lock my room?"

"I didn't lock your room," his mom said.

"Well, I can't get in there. Someone must have locked it."

Max's mom tried to get in the room, but she couldn't. "Maybe something is blocking the door," she said.

Max and his mother went outside and looked in the window to see what was blocking the door. They were amazed at what they saw. All of Max's stuff that he had been leaving everywhere for weeks had fallen in front of the door and was blocking him from getting into his room.

5 minutes

tip

Are you having fun? You cannot expect your students to have fun if you are not having fun with them! If you only read stories like this one about Max like they are boring, standard textbook stories, you will be ineffective. Instead, make your lessons come alive by making them as interactive and engaging as possible. Let your passion for Catholicism shine through each and every day. Enjoy every moment to the fullest and it will not go unnoticed or unappreciated.

We are not at peace with others because we are not at peace with ourselves, and we are not at peace with ourselves because we are not at peace with God

Thomas Merton

111

Step-by-Step

1 Finish reading the story about Max out loud with the class.

When Max's dad came home, he pushed very hard against the door and forced everything to move so Max could climb into his room.

Max spent four hours putting everything away in the right places. He put his clothes in his closet or hamper, he put all his toys away, and he put anything that was trash in the trash can.

When he was finished he promised never to let his room get so messy again.

My Notes:

_____

_____

_____

_____

_____

_____

The deepest desire of our hearts is not to do something or to have something, but rather for peace.

The Rhythm of Life

Just as Max made a mess of his room, sometimes we make a mess in our souls. We leave little sins lying around here and there, and before you know it, they are piling up.

Jesus wants to work with you to tidy up your soul. That's what he is going to do during your First Reconciliation.

5 minutes

tip

Few things endure quite like respect. We don't respect the teachers who let us get away with everything. We respect the teachers who are tough but fair and, at the same time, have our best interests at heart.

You don't have to be worthy; you only have to be willing.

St. Padre Pio

113

WATCH AND DISCUSS

Step-by-Step

1 Introduce Episode 3 by saying: "I never really understood what a sacrament was until I watched this episode."

2 Watch Episode 3.

3 Activity: STRETCH! Guide students in some stretching exercises. Have them stand up and follow your directions for an easy, instant energizer. Try reaching for the ceiling, reaching up and leaning to the right, then leaning left. Have them push their arms straight down without bending and reach toward their toes.

God doesn't ask much of you, just that you cooperate with the grace that he gives you in each moment.

Mustards Seeds

What Is a Sacrament?

A Sacrament is a celebration of God's love for humanity. Through the Sacraments God fills us with the grace we need to become the-best-version-of-ourselves, grow in virtue, and live holy lives.

It is not easy to become the-best-version-of-yourself.

It is not easy to grow in virtue.

It is not easy to live a holy life.

We need God's help. We need God's grace, and the first step is to know that we need it.

My Notes:

_____

_____

_____

_____

_____

_____

_____

Imagine making a journey from New York to San Francisco. You start out walking. It's not difficult to walk down the street, but it's difficult to walk almost three thousand miles from New York to San Francisco.

After a couple of days walking, you think to yourself, "I need a bike." But after a couple of days riding the bike, that doesn't seem so great anymore either. You keep riding and then your parish priest comes along side you and says, "Rachel, what you need is a bus." Along comes a bus and you jump on. It turns out that Jesus is driving the bus. He says, "Hi Rachel, I'm going to help you get there."

The Sacraments and the grace we receive through them are like Jesus' bus. They help us get where we need to go—not to San Francisco, but to heaven.

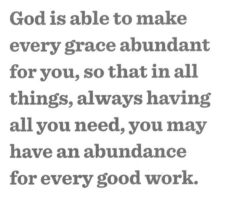

8 minutes

tip

When children are exposed to Jesus, truth, and virtue, they respond with enthusiasm and generosity. In a world that seeks to drown them with the shallow and superficial, most young people discover that a little seriousness is deeply agreeable to their souls.

God is able to make every grace abundant for you, so that in all things, always having all you need, you may have an abundance for every good work.

2 Corinthians 9:8

WATCH AND DISCUSS

Step-by-Step

1 Introduce Episode 4: "This is one of my favorite episodes. I am so excited for you to see it!"

2 Watch Episode 4.

Give your life to God. It is the only thing he desires of you.

Mustards Seeds

What Is Reconciliation?

Well, first, Reconciliation is a Sacrament. So it's one of the ways God blesses us with the grace to become the-best-version-of-ourselves, grow in virtue, and live holy lives.

In particular, Reconciliation is an opportunity to talk to God about the times we have messed up, made poor choices, not been the-best-version-of-ourselves, or turned our backs on God and his wonderful plans for us.

Reconciliation is an opportunity for us to say sorry to him and ask for forgiveness.

It is also an opportunity for the priest to share some ideas about how we can do better in the future. It's like when your coach gives you some tips at halftime about how you can do better. Our priest is one of our spiritual coaches. Great champions listen to their coaches.

We all mess up, and those things can weigh us down. If we don't go to Reconciliation our hearts can become heavy. Through the Sacrament of Reconciliation God forgives our sins and takes the weight of those things off our hearts, so we can live with joy—and share his joy with others.

My Notes:

_____

_____

_____

_____

_____

_____

_____

5 minutes

tip

There is a terrible temptation to allow the story of Jesus to become routine—boring, even. Every illustration in this workbook is a masterpiece, a masterpiece designed to elicit a sense of wonder in your children. Take a moment and ask them to explore this scene in the Gospels. Encourage them to place themselves within the scene. Encourage their imagination and sense of wonder to make the Gospel come alive.

Miss no single opportunity of making some small sacrifice, here by a smiling look, there by a kind word; always doing the smallest right and doing it all for love.

St. Thérèse de Lisieux

WATCH AND DISCUSS

Step-by-Step

1 Before the episode begins, ask: "How does it feel to be the son or daughter of a great King?"

2 Watch Episode 5.

If you don't have time to pray and read the Scriptures, you are busier than God ever intended you to be.

Decision Point

From the Bible: Our Father

You are the son or daughter of a great King. God is that great King. Jesus wanted you to know this. Over and over throughout his life he reminded us that we are children of God.

The disciples often saw Jesus go off to a quiet place to pray. They were curious about prayer and they asked him to teach them how to pray (Matthew 6:9–13).

My Notes:

_____

_____

_____

_____

_____

_____

_____

Jesus taught them to say:

Our Father
Who art in heaven
Hallowed be thy name.
Thy kingdom come,
Thy will be done
On earth as it is in heaven.
Give us this day our daily bread
And forgive us our trespasses.
As we forgive those who trespass against us,
And lead us not into temptation,
But deliver us from evil.

Amen.

Each morning when you wake up, start your day by praying the Our Father. Each night before you go to sleep, end your day by praying the Our Father.

5 minutes

tip
One of the most difficult tasks as a teacher or catechist is handling reluctant and/or disruptive children. Here are some basic tips to help get the most out of these children and to prevent them from negatively influencing the success of the class.

- GIVE THE CHILDREN SOME RESPONSIBILITY, LIKE PASSING OUT THE PENCILS AT THE BEGINNING OF CLASS OR TURNING OUT THE LIGHTS BEFORE EACH ANIMATED EPISODE.

- HELP THEM BE A PART OF THE GROUP BY RECOGNIZING THEM WHEN THEY PARTICIPATE AND APPRECIATING THEIR EFFORTS

- KEEP A SENSE OF HUMOR NO MATTER HOW MUCH THEY TRY YOUR PATIENCE

- BE FIRM AND UNYIELDING BUT FAIR. YOU MAY NOT BE LIKED, BUT YOU WILL BE RESPECTED

Your Father knows what you need before you ask him.

Matthew 6:8

119

WATCH AND DISCUSS

Step-by-Step

1 Give them a preview of the next episode. Tell them: "In this episode, Hemingway gets lost. Let's watch to see if Ben and Sarah find him!" Remember, letting them know you are preparing for your time together matters. They notice.

2 Watch Episode 6.

> When you come to recognize that you are a son or a daughter of God you will also become aware that you lack absolutely nothing.
>
> Mustard Seeds

My Notes:

_____

_____

_____

_____

_____

_____

_____

You Are Blessed

You are the son or daughter of a great King. Jesus wanted us to always remember that God is our Father and that we are children of God.

Now let's say this together:

I am blessed. I am the daughter/son of a great King. He is my Father and my God. The world may praise me or criticize me. It matters not. He is with me, always at my side, guiding and protecting me. I do not fear because I am his.

10 minutes

tip

If you are following the suggested 90-minute format, this marks the approximate halfway point. It is a good time for a brief break. If you are running behind, take a quick look ahead and see where you can get back on track. If ahead of schedule, look for an opportunity in the next 45 minutes to spark a great conversation. If on time, press on and finish strong!

I will be a Father to you and you will be my sons and daughters, says the Lord Almighty.

2 Corinthians 6:18

READ AND EXPLORE

Step-by-Step

1 Read the story of the Good Shepherd aloud.

> When we forgive, we share the love of God with others and rid ourselves of dangerous poisons that can prevent us from growing spiritually.

Rediscover Jesus

The Good Shepherd

Jesus loved to share his wisdom with people by telling stories. One of the stories he told was about a shepherd.

The shepherd had one hundred sheep, and he loved every single one of them and took very good care of them. He made sure they had plenty of food and water, and when the wild wolves came he chased them away from his sheep.

One day one of the sheep got lost. He counted his sheep but only got to ninety-nine. The shepherd was very sad.

So he went out looking for the lost sheep. He looked down by the stream and up in the mountains. Then finally, he heard the sheep crying. It had caught its foot in some wire and couldn't get free.

My Notes:

_____

_____

_____

_____

_____

_____

_____

5 minutes

tip

A child rarely changes his or her behavior or gains new knowledge after hearing something just once. Children need opportunities to repeat activities or to have ideas repeated to reinforce key concepts. That's why throughout this book you will see the text reminding the children that God will never leave them. No matter how many times it is referenced in the text, know that it cannot be overstated. Ever. Throughout your time with your children, constantly remind them of God's unending love for them.

I am the good shepherd. I know my sheep, and they know me. Just as the Father knows me, I know the Father, and I give up my life for my sheep.

John 10:14–15

123

READ AND EXPLORE

Step-by-Step

1 Finish reading the story of the Good Shepherd.

The shepherd carefully removed the sheep's foot from the wire, then picked the sheep up in his arms and carried it all the way home. He was filled with joy that he had found the lost sheep, and he rejoiced.

The shepherd was a very good shepherd. He loved his sheep, and his sheep loved him.

Jesus is the Good Shepherd and we are his sheep. He wants to take care of us. He doesn't want any of us to get lost, but if we do he comes searching for us to save us and bring us home.

Jesus wants to lead us to the home that God the Father has prepared for us in heaven.

Adapted from John 10:1–21

When it comes to heaven, I suspect there will be many surprises. Among these surprises, I think most people will be astounded to learn how much they are loved and how lovable they are.

The Four Signs of a Dynamic Catholic

My Notes:

_____

_____

_____

_____

_____

_____

_____

5 minutes

tip

From time to time, one of your children will ask a question or make a point that will not make sense to the rest of the class. This is a great opportunity for you to offer an example or additional information to ensure that everyone understands. This will get everyone in the room on the same page and will go a long way in showing the child who asked the question that his or her contribution is important.

We are not the sum of our weaknesses and failures; we are the sum of the Father's love for us and our real capacity to become the image of his Son.

St. John Paul II

125

READ AND EXPLORE

Step-by-Step

1 Give the children a moment to explore the illustration, ask questions, and place themselves within the illustration

2 Ask the students: "Will God always love you?" Have the whole class respond, "Yes!" Keep asking until they say it as loudly as they can.

> One of the ways God loves us is by revealing himself to us. He does not remain a distant, anonymous God; he allows us to know him.

Decision Point

126

God Will Always Love You

Like the sheep in the story, we all wander astray from time to time. When we do, it is good to go to Reconciliation and say sorry.

Sometimes when we do the wrong thing we may be tempted to think that some people will not like us anymore. We may even be tempted to think that God will not love us anymore. But that is never true.

God will always love you. There is nothing you can do that will make him stop loving you. We all make mistakes, we all mess up, and we all make poor choices from time to time. But God never stops loving us. You need to always remember this.

You may think you have done something horrible and God will never forgive you. But that is stinking thinking. God doesn't want you to think like that. He is always willing to forgive us when we are sorry, and there is nothing you can do that will cause him to stop loving you.

God loves you so much. He loves you so much that he wants to help you every day and in every way to become the-best-version-of-yourself!

My Notes:

_____

_____

_____

_____

_____

_____

_____

5 minutes

Right now, it is part of your mission to inspire your children, or at least lead them to inspiration; to show them new possibilities; to capture their imaginations; and to show them they are capable of things they dare not even dream of.

Let no one mourn that he has fallen again and again: for forgiveness has risen from the grave!

St. John Chrysostom

127

Step-by-Step

1 Have your children complete the activity page by themselves, with a partner, or as a group.

2 After three minutes, ask the class: "Are there any questions you are struggling with?"

3 Briefly explain the answer to any questions they might have, referring back to the specific page in the workbook.

Life is a long journey. Every day we come to many forks in the road, and we have to decide which path we will walk.

Decision Point

Show What You Know

True or False

1. __T__ Forgiveness is essential to healthy relationships. (p 107)

2. __F__ God doesn't forgive us. (p 126)

3. __F__ God gives us confession so we can feel bad about ourselves. (p 109)

4. __T__ Your priest is one of your spiritual coaches. (p 116)

5. __T__ God is always willing to forgive you. (p 126)

Fill in the blank

1. God delights in a healthy __relationship__ with you and others. (p 107)

2. God invites you to become the-best-version-of-yourself because he wants you to live a holy life and be __happy__. (p 106)

3. In relationships two of the most important life lessons are: how to __forgive__ and how to be __forgiven__. (p 107)

4. In the __Our Father__ we pray, "forgive us our trespasses as we forgive those who trespass against us." (p 107)

5. Because we all sin, God blesses us with the Sacrament of __Reconciliation__ so we can live with joy and share his joy with others. (p 108)

My Notes:

_____

_____

_____

_____

_____

_____

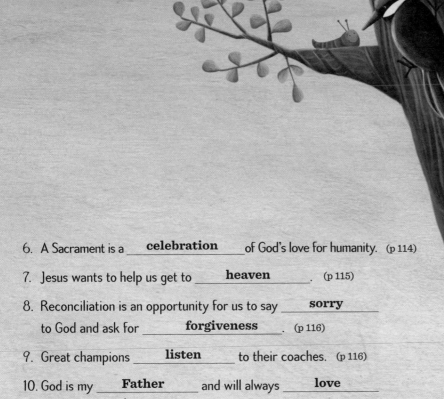

6. A Sacrament is a __celebration__ of God's love for humanity. (p 114)

7. Jesus wants to help us get to __heaven__. (p 115)

8. Reconciliation is an opportunity for us to say __sorry__ to God and ask for __forgiveness__. (p 116)

9. Great champions __listen__ to their coaches. (p 116)

10. God is my __Father__ and will always __love__ me no matter what. (p 126)

Word Bank

LOVE	FORGIVE	LISTEN	SORRY	FATHER	FORGIVEN	RECONCILIATION
HAPPY	HEAVEN	FORGIVENESS	RELATIONSHIP	OUR FATHER	CELEBRATION	

10 minutes

tip

If you are willing to surrender and to serve God by serving others in ministry, you will see miracles. You may not literally witness the lame walk or the blind see, but metaphorically you will see these and much greater things. The life of a teacher and catechist is one of sacrifice, but those sacrifices give birth to everyday miracles.

Nothing great is ever achieved without enduring much.

St. Catherine of Siena

JOURNAL WITH JESUS

Step-by-Step

1 Invite your children to write a letter to Jesus.

2 Ask the children to remain silent during their journaling time.

3 You may wish to play some quiet, reflective music to help create the right mood in the classroom and to encourage the students to remain quiet and focused on journaling with Jesus.

You can search the whole world for happiness, but it will elude you until you realize that it is only by bringing happiness to others that we ever find happiness for ourselves.

Decision Point

My Notes:

_____

_____

_____

_____

_____

_____

_____

Journal with Jesus

Dear Jesus,

I know you will always love me because . . .

_____

_____

_____

_____

_____

_____

_____

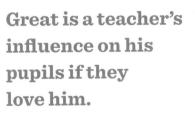

5 minutes

_____

_____

_____

_____

_____

_____

_____

tip
Routine is beautiful.
We spend a lot of our lives
rebelling against it, but the
truth is routines bring out
the best in us. Encourage the
children to develop healthy
routines in their lives and to
make journaling one of them.

Great is a teacher's influence on his pupils if they love him.

St. John Bosco

CLOSING PRAYER

Step-by-Step

1 Introduce Episode 7 by saying: "We are about to hear the story of David fighting the mighty Goliath. It is one of the most famous stories in the whole Bible for a reason: It is an amazing story!"

2 Watch Episode 7.

The saints were not born saints, and they weren't perfect. They were men and women like you and me who realized that the world's vision for them was bankrupt, so they turned to God and his vision for their lives. You can do that too.

Decision Point

Closing Prayer

Since the beginning of time, God has been using ordinary people to accomplish extraordinary things. King David is just one example. He came from a big family, and as a child he worked in the fields as a shepherd boy.

One day David brought lunch to his seven brothers who were on the battlefield defending Israel against the Philistines. David arrived and heard the giant Goliath making fun of the Israelites and God. Goliath was the Philistines' greatest warrior and he thought he was more powerful than God. Everyone was afraid of Goliath and refused to fight him.

Believing in the power of God's protection, David volunteered to fight Goliath. God gave David great courage and helped him to slay Goliath. No one believed that young David could defeat the great warrior Goliath. But anything is possible with God.

Later in his life, after King Saul died, David became King of Israel. Until Jesus, David was the greatest king in Israel's history. But David was not perfect. When David made himself available to God great things happened. When he closed himself off to God his life started to fall apart. With God he was happy. When he turned away from God he was miserable.

Adapted from 1 Samuel 17 and 2 Samuel 4–5

My Notes:

_____

_____

_____

_____

_____

_____

3 minutes

The biggest Christian lie in history is not one that others tell about us. It is a lie we tell ourselves: holiness is not possible. This lie neutralizes our Christianity. It is diabolical. Holiness is possible. God uses the most unlikely people to do his greatest work. He almost never uses those in positions of power and authority; he doesn't necessarily use the most educated, or the best looking, or even the most qualified. Whom does God use to do his most powerful work here on earth? He uses the people who make themselves available to him. How available are you to God? 10 percent, 50 percent, 95 percent? Or are you 100 percent available for whatever God calls you to today? If you want to see something incredible happen in your life and in the lives of your children, make yourself available to God.

Do not spend your energies on things that generate worry, anxiety and anguish. Only one thing is necessary: Lift up your spirit and love God.

St. Padre Pio

133

CLOSING PRAYER

Step-by-Step

1 Ask the children: "What are some of the most important things you learned in this session?"

- GOD LOVES HEALTHY RELATIONSHIPS.
- FORGIVENESS IS ESSENTIAL TO HEALTHY RELATIONSHIPS.
- RECONCILIATION CLEANS UP THE MESS IN MY SOUL.
- GOD IS ALWAYS WILLING TO FORGIVE US WHEN WE ARE SORRY.
- JESUS WANTS TO LEAD US TO HEAVEN.
- I AM GOD'S SON/ DAUGHTER.
- GOD CHOOSES ORDINARY PEOPLE TO ACCOMPLISH EXTRAORDINARY THINGS.

Whom does God use to do his most powerful work here on earth? He uses the people who make themselves available to him.

Decision Point

King David recognized these patterns of happiness and misery in his life. He learned that when he allowed God to lead him, like he used to lead the sheep in the pastures as a child, he was happiest. With this wisdom he wrote one of the most famous prayers of all time. It is called Psalm 23:

> The Lord is my shepherd, there is nothing I shall want;
> he lets me lay down in green pastures.
> He leads me beside peaceful waters;
> he restores my soul.
> He leads me in paths of righteousness for his name's sake.
> Even though I walk through the valley of the shadow of death,
> I will not be afraid; for he is with me;
> his rod and thy staff, they comfort and protect me.
> He prepares a table before me in the presence of my enemies;
> he anoints my head with oil, my cup overflows.
> Surely goodness and mercy will follow me all the days of my life;
> and I will live in the house of the Lord forever.
>
> Amen.

My Notes:

_____

_____

_____

_____

_____

_____

_____

_____

2 minutes

tip

Share with your children one way in which your life has changed because you have granted forgiveness or been forgiven.

Prayer gives us light by which to see and to judge from God's perspective and from eternity. That is why you must not give up on praying!

St. John Paul II

5

Your First Reconciliation

QUICK SESSION OVERVIEW

Opening Prayer. . . . . 2 min

Watch and Discuss; Read and Explore . . . . .71 min

Show What You Know . . . . 10 min

Journal with Jesus. . . . . 5 min

Closing Prayer. . . . . 2 min

OBJECTIVES

- **TO DEMONSTRATE** that Reconciliation is a lifelong blessing.

- **TO EXPLAIN** that, no matter how far we may wander from God, he will never stop searching for us and he will never stop encouraging us to become the-best-version-ourselves, grow in virtue, and live holy lives.

- **TO TEACH** that their First Reconciliation is going to be a great moment in their lives.

- # A healing gift.
- # A chance to start all over again.

① WELCOME

Helping young people find and walk the path toward God is not easy. They will wear you out at times and frustrate you beyond belief at others. That's why it's critical to stay in touch with your why.

Why are you here? Why is it important to you that your candidates discover the genius of Catholicism? Why are you passionate about helping these young people develop a rich faith life? The more you stay connected with your "why," the more passionate you will be. Take a few minutes to reflect on this before each class. It will unleash new energy within you.

Remind yourself to smile. Welcome them. Tell them you missed them and have been thinking about them.

Prayer Icon

Read and Explore

Watch and Discuss

Show What You Know

Journal with Jesus

Time Tracker

OPENING PRAYER

Step-by-Step

1. Take a moment to get your children quiet and settled down.

2. Pray the opening prayer.

Life is too short to be lived halfheartedly and far too short to lose yourself in the day-to-day drudgery and the hustle and bustle.

The Rhythm of Life

My Notes:

5

Your First Reconciliation

God, our loving Father,
thank you for all the ways you bless me.
Help me to be aware that every person,
place, and adventure I experience is an
opportunity to love you more.
Fill me with a desire to change and to grow,
and give me the wisdom to choose
the-best-version-of-myself in
every moment of every day.

Amen.

🕐
2 minutes

tip
Speak to the candidates about why quiet time is important in our lives. Encourage them to continue the habit of taking a few quiet minutes in prayer each day for the rest of their lives. Remind them that there are going to be tough times in their lives and times when they are confused, and encourage them at those times in particular to turn to God in prayer and to ask him to guide them.

Begin with the Sign of the Cross. Then invite them to close their eyes and read the opening prayer slowly and deliberately.

**Because he
bends down
to listen,
I will pray
as long as
I have breath.**

Psalm 116:2

137

WATCH AND DISCUSS

Step-by-Step

1 Watch Episode 1.

2 In Episode 1, Tiny experiences a great moment. After the episode, have the children share a great moment in their lives: a favorite birthday, the first goal in soccer, a new pet, etc. Don't hesitate to share one of your own great moments.

The challenge is to learn to have fun doing the things that matter most.

The Rhythm of Life

Great Moments in Life

Life is full of great moments. When you were born, that was a great moment. Christmas, Easter, feast days, and birthdays are all great moments.

The first time you score a goal in soccer is a great moment. The day you graduate from college is a great moment. Getting your first job is a great moment. Discovering your vocation is a great moment.

My Notes:

_____

_____

_____

_____

_____

_____

_____

Ordinary moments can be great too—like a beautiful sunset, a fabulous meal with family, or meeting a new friend.

Your First Reconciliation is going to be one of the great moments of your life.

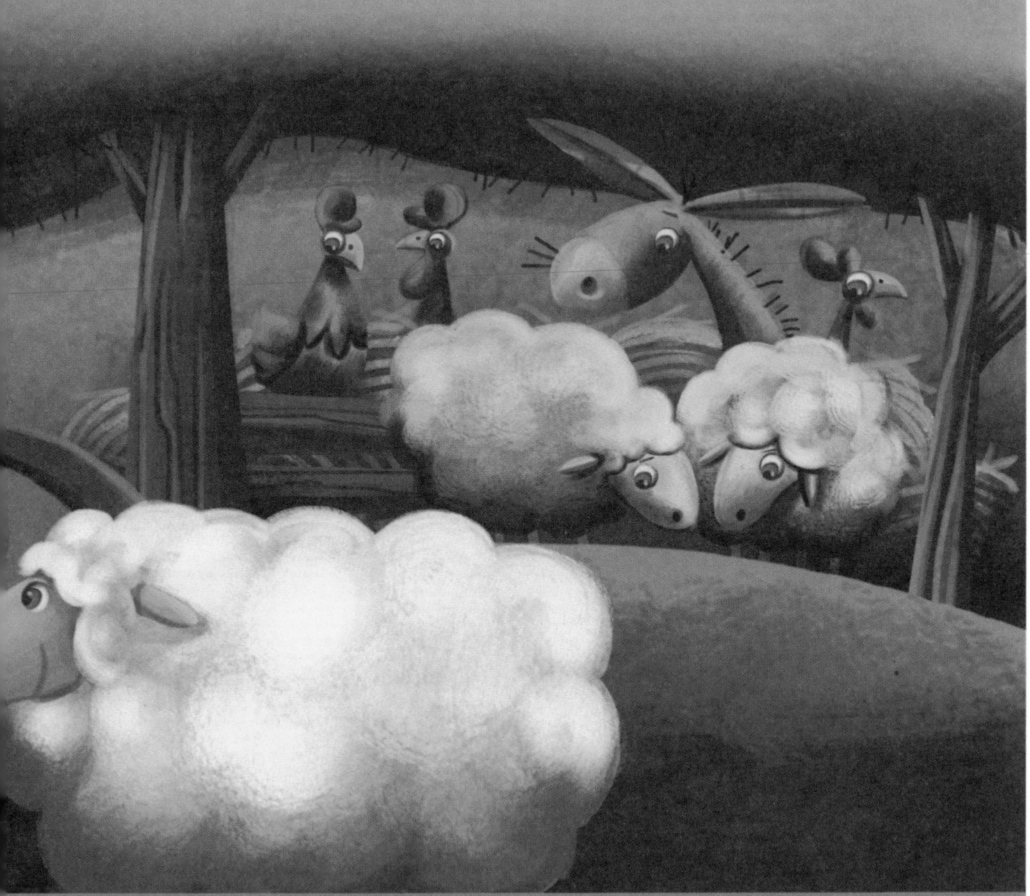

5 minutes

tip

One of the ugliest things in the world is a person who has lost joy in trying to serve other people. Joy is at the heart of any service we perform for another person. Service without joy is ugly. So, why have you decided to lead this class? Your why and your joy are connected. If you've lost your why, there is no better time to get it back.

Remember . . . that nothing is small in the eyes of God. Do all that you do with love.

St. Thérèse de Lisieux

READ AND EXPLORE

Step-by-Step

1 Take a moment for self-discovery. Give the children a few moments to examine the artwork. Encourage them to recognize the beautiful flowers and the fabulous fountain. Then ask them: "Is there anything out of place here? Is there anything that doesn't seem to fit in this beautiful garden? That's right, the ugly, nasty, terrible thorn bush!"

2 Then, read the text aloud with a bit of drama. It's a great story, so make sure you are having some fun with it!

We live our lives for an audience of one: God.

Resisting Happiness

The Garden of Your Heart

Imagine you are in a beautiful garden. It is springtime and the grass is green, the sun is shining, the flowers are blossoming with bright colors, butterflies are fluttering, bees are buzzing, and the birds are happily chirping.

Then you notice some nasty weeds and overgrown thornbushes over by the edge of the garden.

My Notes:

_____

_____

_____

_____

_____

_____

Now the gardener comes. He waters all the flowers, sings with the birds, enjoys the sunshine, and pets a rabbit that hops by. As the gardener makes his way around the garden he notices what you noticed: the nasty weeds and overgrown thornbushes. He doesn't get angry; he just smiles lovingly and gets to work. He carefully pulls out the weeds and removes the thornbushes. Then he tills the soil and plants some seeds so that this area can be as beautiful as the rest of the garden.

5 minutes

In the same way, let your light shine before others, that they may see your good deeds and glorify your Father in heaven.

Matthew 5:16

READ AND EXPLORE

Step-by-Step

1 Read the rest of the text aloud.

2 When you say the words, "Jesus is the gardener," be sure to exclaim with excitement and surprise. These children will follow your lead. If you are excited and surprised, they will be too.

Find something good in each person you meet and help it to grow.

Mustard Seeds

The garden in this story is your heart. The beautiful flowers in the garden are the love you carry in your heart for God and for your family and friends.

Every time you make a good choice, the garden becomes even more beautiful. Every time you help a friend or a stranger, a flower blooms. Each time you choose to listen to your parents, the grass gets a little bit greener. But every time you push someone on the playground or cut in front of someone at the drinking fountain, a weed grows in your garden. And each time you tell a lie or say a bad word, the thornbush begins to grow.

My Notes:

_____
_____
_____
_____
_____
_____
_____

Jesus is the gardener. He wants to live in your heart. He loves walking in your garden, enjoying the beauty of your heart. He also wants to remove all the weeds and thornbushes from your garden. The weeds are the small sins; the thornbushes are your big sins. If you don't get rid of the weeds and thornbushes as soon as they start to grow, they can spread very quickly and take over the whole garden.

In the Sacrament of Reconciliation we invite Jesus the gardener to come into the garden of our hearts and remove all the weeds and thornbushes.

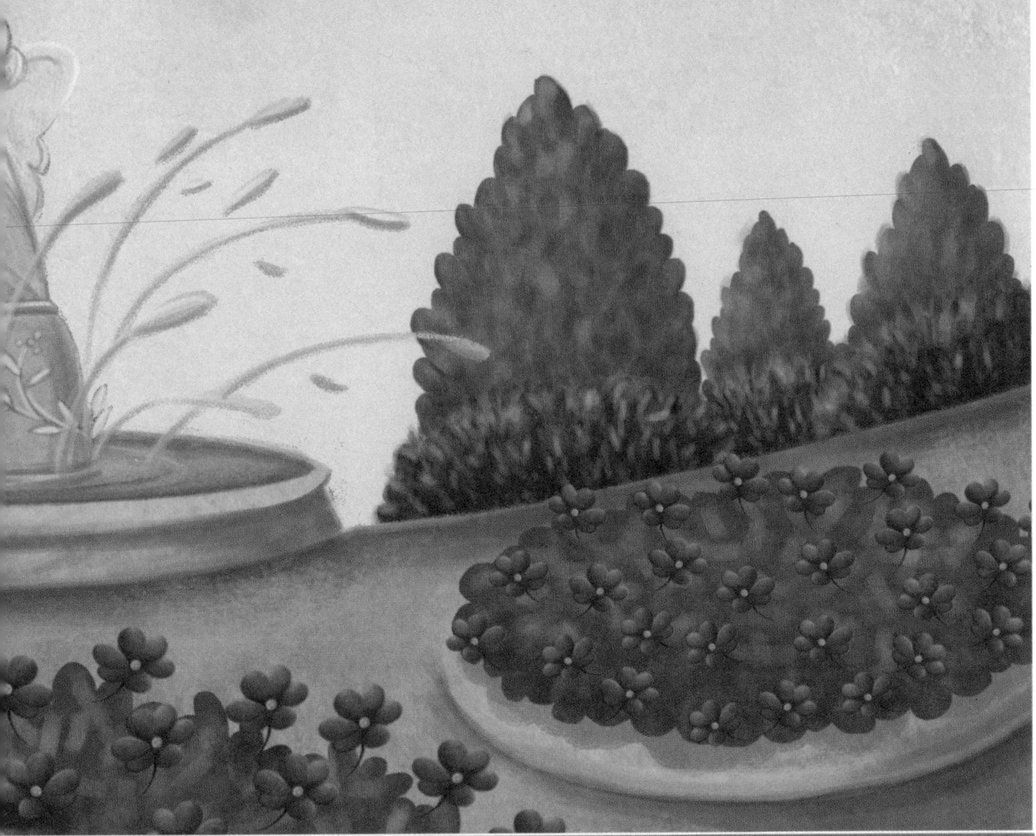

3 minutes

tip

Remember, repetition is a powerful learning tool, so when you are done reading, ask your children: "Who is the gardener of your heart?" Don't let them get away with mumbling "Jesus" or saying it quietly. Keep asking until they say it loud and proud!

I have told you these things, so that you have peace.

John 16:33

WATCH AND DISCUSS

Step-by-Step

1 Introduce the episodes by saying, "We prepare for all of life's greatest moments, and here's why . . ."

2 Watch Episodes 2 and 3.

3 Activity: MUSICAL CHAIRS Set chairs in two rows back-to-back with one fewer chair than the number of players. Begin to play music, and have the children walk in a circle around the chairs. At a time of your choosing, pause the music. When the music stops, each child races to sit in an available chair. There should be one child without a chair to sit in. That child is out. Repeat the process until there is only one child left or until 3 minutes have passed.

Dreams come true when opportunity and preparation meet.

The Rhythm of Life

Preparation Matters

We prepare for everything important.

You wouldn't expect to win a big soccer tournament if you hadn't been practicing. You cannot expect good grades if you don't study for your exams. You wouldn't go on a trip without packing and planning. Preparation is essential for a great experience.

My Notes:

You are blessed to be Catholic. As Catholics we prepare for each of the Catholic Moments. We prepare for Christmas with the season of Advent. We prepare for Easter with the season of Lent. We prepare for Mass with prayer and fasting.

You have been preparing for your First Reconciliation. As that wonderful day gets closer, there are some final preparations to be made.

12 minutes

tip
Encourage the children; some of your candidates may have no genuine encouragement in their lives.

> **Every moment we live through is like an ambassador that declares the will of God to us.**
>
> Jean Pierre de Caussade

READ AND EXPLORE

Step-by-Step

1 Have a different child read aloud the 5 steps to making a great Reconciliation.

> **Wisdom is not the amassing of knowledge. Wisdom is truth lived.**
>
> The Rhythm of Life

The Five Steps

You are preparing for your First Reconciliation. This will be your first time, but not your last time. You are blessed.

The second time you go to Reconciliation you will know what to do because you will have done it before. But because this is your first time, it makes sense to walk through exactly what will happen.

Let's take a step-by-step look at the Sacrament of Reconciliation so you can know how it works. Then we will talk about each step in detail so you will know what to expect.

First, it is natural to be a little nervous. The first time we do most things we feel nervous. It's like riding a roller coaster: The first time you are really nervous, but the more times you ride it, the less nervous you become.

My Notes:

_____

_____

_____

_____

_____

_____

_____

There are five steps to making a great Reconciliation. Here is a quick overview.

Step 1: Examination of Conscience

This is a spiritual exercise designed to help us remember when we were and when we were not the-best-version-of-ourselves. By examining our conscience we become aware of our sins.

Step 2: Confession

Here we say sorry to God by confessing our sins to him through the priest who is God's representative.

Step 3: Penance

The priest will ask you to spend some time in prayer or to do a kind deed for somebody. This is called penance, which is a way for you to show God that you are truly sorry for your sins.

Step 4: Contrition

The Act of Contrition is a short prayer we pray promising to try not to sin again.

Step 5: Absolution

The priest will then extend his hands over your head and pray a very special and powerful prayer. Acting as God's representative, he will forgive your sins!

5 minutes

tip

In general, most of your children are going to be nervous for their First Reconciliation. It's a new experience, and for children this age, new experiences are often a bit frightening. Take a moment and share with them about your First Reconciliation. Were you nervous? How did you feel afterward? How do you feel about Reconciliation now?

Confession is an act of honesty and courage—an act of entrusting ourselves, beyond sin, to the mercy of a loving and forgiving God.

St. John Paul II

WATCH AND DISCUSS

Step-by-Step

1 Introduce the next episode by asking: "Have you ever wondered what happens during Reconciliation? Well, this episode is about to tell us."

2 Watch Episode 4.

Develop a strong, uncompromising commitment to becoming the-best-version-of-yourself. Make the decisions of your life with that purpose and goal in mind.

The Rhythm of Life

Step 1: We Examine Our Conscience

To help you become the-best-version-of-yourself and live a holy life, God has blessed you with a conscience, the gentle voice inside you that encourages you to do good and avoid evil. God speaks to us through our conscience.

Following our conscience makes us happy. Ignoring our conscience makes us irritable, restless, and unhappy.

My Notes:

_____

_____

_____

_____

_____

_____

_____

God doesn't want us to be restless and unhappy, so he gives us the gift of Reconciliation. When we disobey our conscience and sin by doing things that we know we shouldn't do, God invites us to come to Reconciliation so that he can fill us with his joy again.

Before we go to Reconciliation we examine our conscience so that we know what to talk to the priest about. To examine means to look at something very carefully.

Imagine you had a beautiful big diamond and you carried it with you everywhere you went. From time to time you would probably take it out and look at it. If it was very dusty or dirty, you would clean it. If it had a scratch, you would polish it.

Your soul is that beautiful diamond. We come to Reconciliation so God can dust, clean, and polish it so that it can shine like new again.

15 minutes

tip

If you are following the suggested 90-minute format, this marks the approximate halfway point. It is a good time for a brief break. If you are running behind, take a quick look ahead and see where you can get back on track. If ahead of schedule, look for an opportunity in the next 45 minutes to spark a great conversation. If on time, press on and finish strong!

True happiness, dear friends, does not consist in the pleasures of the world or in earthly things, but in peace of conscience.

Blessed Pierre Giorgio Frassati

Step-by-Step

1 Have a different child read each of the examine questions out loud.

Before you go to Reconciliation it helps to think back and remember any times that you have chosen to sin, walked down a wrong path, made a poor choice, broken one of God's commandments, not listened to your conscience, or simply not been the-best-version-of-yourself.

These questions may help you to examine your conscience:

Have I been a good friend?

Do I obey my parents?

Have I taken things that belong to other people?

Do I cheat in school or in sports?

Have I told any lies?

Do I take time to pray each day?

Have I used God's name in ways that are not appropriate?

Do I go to church each Sunday?

Am I grateful for the many gifts that God has blessed me with?

The answers to these questions will help you to prepare for the Sacrament of Reconciliation. By taking time to reflect on the questions you will be prepared to speak to the priest when you enter the Reconciliation room.

It's hard for us to remember all the times we have sinned; that's why an examination of conscience is helpful. Sitting in a quiet place and thinking through questions like these will help you to remember times when you have not been the-best-version-of-yourself.

My Notes:

_____

_____

_____

_____

_____

_____

_____

Silence has been a great friend to the extraordinary men and women of every age.

The Rhythm of Life

2 minutes

tip

Feel free to walk around during the discussions. This will help to hold their attention. If someone is speaking, move a little closer to him or her. This helps them to know that you are curious and interested in what they have to say. If someone is not on task or is misbehaving, move closer to him or her. This proximity control is a good nonverbal way to capture attention.

The examination of conscience never induces despair, always hope . . . because examination of conscience is done in the light of God's love.

Venerable Fulton J. Sheen

151

READ AND EXPLORE

Step-by-Step

1 Read the story of Daniel out loud. Ask if one of the students would like to play the role of Daniel's mother and read her lines aloud.

God has a better plan than any you can put together for yourself.

Decision Point

152

Step 2: We Confess Our Sins

Daniel really loved cookies. One afternoon, he came home from school and his mom was baking a fresh batch of his favorite kind, chocolate chip. The whole house smelled delicious! As he walked into the kitchen his mom said, "Daniel, I know these are your favorite cookies, but I am baking this batch for the church picnic. So, you may only have one." As his mother's back was turned, Daniel quickly grabbed two cookies and ran to his room.

He gobbled down the cookies. They tasted yummy in his mouth, but they left him feeling yucky inside. He knew he had done the wrong thing. Even though he hadn't been caught, he felt terrible.

My Notes:

_____

_____

_____

_____

_____

_____

_____

Daniel was embarrassed, but his conscience encouraged him to go and tell his mother what he had done and to say sorry. His mother gave him a big hug and said, "I am disappointed in you for doing something you knew was wrong, and as a punishment tonight you cannot watch your favorite TV show. But Daniel, I also want you to know that I am very proud of you for saying sorry and admitting that you did the wrong thing. That took a lot of courage."

When the kids in Daniel's class were preparing for their First Reconciliation they asked themselves lots of questions during the examination of conscience. He remembered when he took the extra cookie. He knew it was good that he had apologized to his mom, but he also needed to say sorry to God for stealing. He realized this was something he could confess during Reconciliation.

5 minutes

tip

Many people who are good at leading are left-brain people. We like problems we can solve; we like answers; we like order; we like things to be in their place. But helping young people enter into a powerful relationship with Jesus and his Church can be messy. The path is different for every candidate. They all have different questions, struggles, doubts, and hopes. Be flexible. It's okay if every session does not go as you planned. Let the Holy Spirit guide you and these classes.

Our hearts were made for you, O Lord, and they are restless until they rest in you.

St. Augustine

153

READ AND EXPLORE

Step-by-Step

1 Read the text aloud.

When you enter the Reconciliation room or confessional, you will sit in a chair across from the priest. After you make the Sign of the Cross it is time for you to confess your sins. You tell the priest about your sins. Remember Daniel from our story? This is when he would talk to the priest about the time he stole the cookie. If you get stuck or nervous, remember, the priest is there to help you.

By talking with the priest about the times that we made poor choices and the times we were not the-best-version-of-ourselves, we rediscover the person God created us to be.

The priest may make some suggestions about how you can grow and become a better person. Remember, although you are sitting with the priest, he is there to represent God. So you are really telling God.

My Notes:

_____

_____

_____

_____

_____

_____

_____

Who are you getting your spiritual coaching from?

Decision Point

It is also possible to receive this Sacrament behind a screen. The priest sits on the other side of the screen and listens to you as you kneel and confess your sins.

Great champions listen to their coaches so they can get better. Reconciliation is a type of spiritual coaching. Confessing our sins to God is a beautiful way to grow spiritually.

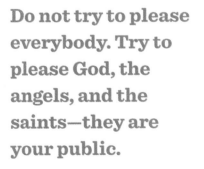

2 minutes

tip

Talk a little about the courage Daniel must have needed to admit the wrong he had done. Share about a time in your life when you needed courage to admit when you were wrong.

Do not try to please everybody. Try to please God, the angels, and the saints—they are your public.

St. John Vianney

Step-by-Step

1 Ask the children how they would feel if they ate two dozen donuts.

Step 3: We Perform Our Penance

If you ate two dozen donuts every day for a few months, you would become quite sick. While you were eating all those donuts you probably knew that they were not good for you, but you kept eating them anyway.

Then one day you woke up and you came to your senses. You realized that eating all those donuts was making you sick. It's good to be sorry, but it is equally important to change the way we live.

If you had been eating all those donuts and your body was sick, you would need to exercise and eat plenty of fruits and vegetables so your body could get healthy again.

Sin makes our soul sick like bad food makes our body sick. When we go to Reconciliation we say sorry for offending God and making our soul sick, but we also promise to try to live differently in the future.

Before we recite our Act of Contrition, the priest will give us a penance. Penance is a prayer or kind deed that we do to show God that we are really sorry. It is like exercise for the soul to help it get healthy again.

My Notes:

_____

_____

_____

_____

_____

_____

_____

> Love is a choice, not a feeling—and it's a choice that proves itself with action.

Decision Point

156

tip

When you live out the faith, people will want to be with you and the children will want to listen to you. Why? It will no longer be you living and teaching, but Christ living and teaching in you.

A tree is known by its fruit; a man by his deeds. A good deed is never lost; he who sows courtesy reaps friendship, and he who plants kindness gathers love.

St. Basil

READ AND EXPLORE

Step-by-Step

1 Read aloud the two examples of the Act of Contrition.

2 Have the children practice reading the first Act of Contrition out loud. The more comfortable they feel with the Act of Contrition, the more comfortable they will be on the day of their First Reconciliation.

What you do now is going to matter later in your life in ways that you have not even begun to imagine.

Decision Point

Step 4: We Say Sorry to God

Rachel was angry with her sister. Each time she sat down to do her homework, her sister would bother her, and today Rachel lost her temper and pushed her away. Her sister fell down and started to cry. She had just wanted Rachel to play with her. Rachel felt bad about her choice and apologized to her sister. To show her sister she was really sorry, Rachel said that after she finished her homework she would play any game her sister chose.

After you confess your sins in the Sacrament of Reconciliation, you will pray a prayer of contrition. What is contrition? Contrition means to be sorry. When you pray the words in the prayer of contrition, you are telling God that you are truly sorry for the sins that you have committed.

Here are two examples of an Act of Contrition:

Dear God, I am sorry for all my sins. I am sorry for the wrong things I have done. I am sorry for the good things I have failed to do. I will do better with your help. Amen.

My God, I am sorry for my sins with all my heart. In choosing to do wrong and failing to do good, I have sinned against you whom I should love above all things. I firmly intend, with your help, to do penance, to sin no more, and to avoid whatever leads me to sin. Our Savior Jesus Christ suffered and died for us. In his name, my God, have mercy.

Amen.

My Notes:

_____

_____

_____

_____

_____

_____

_____

2 minutes

tip

Tell your children why you love going to Reconciliation. Remind them that their First Reconciliation is a big deal, whether or not they realize it yet.

Cast yourself into the arms of God and be very sure that if he wants anything of you, he will fit you for the work and give you the strength.

St. Philip Neri

READ AND EXPLORE

Step-by-Step

1 Read the text aloud.

2 Ask the students how they felt when they watched the episode with Jesus in the confessional forgiving sins through the priest. Were they amazed, confused, grateful, excited?

Love is the core of Jesus' philosophy. But in order to love you must be free. For to love is to give yourself freely and without reservation.

Rediscover Catholicism

Step 5: The Priest Offers Us Absolution

After the Last Supper, Jesus knew he was going to suffer and die, but he also knew why. He was doing it for you and me, so we could be free from our sins.

Sin makes us unhappy and feels heavy. Jesus didn't want us to feel this way. He wanted us to be free from sin. He wanted us to be able to go to Reconciliation and have our sins forgiven.

My Notes:

_____

_____

_____

_____

_____

_____

_____

_____

After you recite the Act of Contrition the priest will stretch his hands over your head to pray this prayer of absolution:

God, the Father of Mercies, through the death and resurrection of his Son, has reconciled the world to himself and sent the Holy Spirit among us for the forgiveness of sins; through the ministry of the Church may God give you pardon and peace, and I absolve you from your sins in the name of the Father, and of the Son, and of the Holy Spirit.

You will respond: **Amen**.

At the moment of absolution, as the priest extends his hands over you, Jesus is pouring his grace upon you. This is like a bucket of love pouring down upon your head and filling your heart with peace and joy. God's grace also empowers you to make better choices.

After the priest has absolved you of your sins, he will send you forth to walk with God more closely, make better choices, and become the-best-version-of-yourself.

5 minutes

tip

The closer you get to the end of the class, the more restless some of your children will become. Be prepared for that; have techniques at the ready. Take a break and play a song or a game. Think of ways to actively keep them engaged until the end.

His mercies never come to an end; they are new every morning.

Lamentations 3:22-23

161

WATCH AND DISCUSS

Step-by-Step

1 Introduce the next episode: "The Prodigal Son is one of the most famous stories in the entire Bible. It is about how God the Father always rejoices when we return home to him."

2 Watch Episode 5.

**Ask yourself...
if I lived one
Gospel reading
100%, how much
would my life
change?**

Decision Point

From the Bible: The Prodigal Son

Once upon a time there was a man who had two sons. The younger son came to his father one day and said, "Father, give me the share of your money that will belong to me." The father agreed and a few days later his younger son left and travelled to a distant land, where he wasted all the money on frivolous things.

Soon he had no money and was hungry, so he took a job feeding pigs. He was so hungry he wanted to eat the pigs' food.

My Notes:

_____

_____

_____

_____

_____

_____

_____

One day he was feeding the pigs and he thought to himself, "My father's servants have plenty of food to eat and I am starving. I will go back home, beg my father to forgive me, and ask him to take me back, not as a son but as his servant."

The next day he set off and went to his father. When he was still a far way from home, his father saw him on the horizon. The father was filled with joy and he ran to greet his son, wrapping his arms around him and kissing him.

3 minutes

Whenever you feel unloved, unimportant, or insecure, remember to whom you belong.

Ephesians 2:19–22

READ AND EXPLORE

Step-by-Step

1 Read the last three paragraphs out loud to the children. Read slowly and deliberately. Let the tone and inflection of your voice tell them: this is something worth listening to.

The son said to his father, "Father, I have sinned against heaven and against you. I am no longer worthy to be called your son. Take me back as a servant." But the father said to his servants, "Quickly, bring out a robe—the best one—and put it on him; put a ring on his finger and sandals on his feet. And get the fatted calf and prepare it so that we can eat and have a great celebration. For this son of mine was lost but now he is found; he was dead, but now he is alive."

Adapted from Luke 15: 11–32

God is always waiting on us. Sometimes we may think we are waiting on him, but that is never true.

Rediscover Jesus

My Notes:

_____

_____

_____

_____

_____

_____

_____

Jesus loved to teach in parables because each person in the story teaches us a lesson. In this parable, the father is God the Father. He always rejoices when we return to him. He is not angry with his son; he is delighted that the boy has come home.

There may be times in your life when you feel far from God. But never think that God does not want you to return home. Never think that your sins are greater than God's love.

The son in this story is called the Prodigal Son. Prodigal means "careless and foolish." We are all careless and foolish at times. When we sin we are being careless and foolish. But when we come to Reconciliation we are like the son returning home to his father, and his father rejoices.

2 minutes

tip

If your children leave the First Reconciliation preparation process remembering just one thing, let it be this: God will always love them, he will always be calling them back home to him, and his love will always be bigger than their sin. Remind them of this constantly.

> We have been called to heal wounds, to unite what has fallen away, and to bring home those who have lost their way.
>
> St. Francis of Assisi

WATCH AND DISCUSS

Step-by-Step

1 Introduce Episode 6 by asking the children: "Do you think this will be the first and only time you ever go to Reconciliation?"

2 Watch Episode 6.

Make a commitment to do something every day for the rest of your life that will help you grow spiritually.

Decision Point

First, but Not Last

Reconciliation is a great blessing. You are blessed.

This is your First Reconciliation, but not your last. It is a good idea to get comfortable with the process. It is natural and normal to be nervous, especially the first time. But if you go regularly you will become more comfortable.

Regular Reconciliation is one of the best ways God shares his grace with us. Many of the saints went every month, some even more often.

My Notes:

_____

_____

_____

_____

_____

_____

_____

Going to Reconciliation regularly reminds us of how important it is to focus on growing spiritually and not just physically.

To become the-best-version-of-yourself, grow in virtue, and live a holy life is a lifelong process. Daily prayer, Sunday Mass, and regular Reconciliation are three ways that guide and encourage us in that journey.

3 minutes

tip

The day of their First Reconciliation is quickly approaching. Mention it from time to time. Tell them you are excited for them. Building anticipation is essential to having a memorable experience.

No one was ever lost because his sin was too great, but because his trust was too small.

Blessed Francis Xavier Seelos

READ AND EXPLORE

Step-by-Step

1 Ask the children: "Who is the best friend you will ever have?"

Jesus is the friend you have been yearning for your whole life.

Rediscover Jesus

Your Best Friend

Friendship is beautiful, but it is also fragile. Sometimes a friend may do things that upset us. This weakens our friendship with him or her. But when that friend says sorry, our friendship is repaired and even strengthened.

God is the best friend you will ever have. Sometimes we do things that offend him. This weakens our friendship with him. We come to the Sacrament of Reconciliation to say sorry to God.

There may be times when you wander away from God. But God will never stop calling to you. He will never stop searching for you. God will never stop encouraging you to become the-best-version-of-yourself, grow in virtue, and live a holy life.

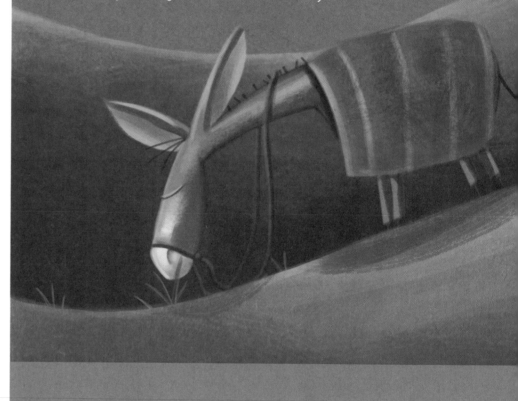

My Notes:

_____

_____

_____

_____

_____

_____

_____

1 minutes

tip

The illustration depicts the story of the Good Samaritan. If time allows, read this story from Luke 10:25–37 in your Bible. Tell the children that this is the kind of friend God encourages us to be.

Since it is your responsibility to teach your students about God, you must first become aware of the action of God in your life. Teach by example. Put into practice what you want your students to believe.

St. John Baptist de La Salle

SHOW WHAT YOU KNOW

Step-by-Step

1 Have your children complete the activity page by themselves, with a partner, or as a group.

2 After three minutes ask the class, "Are there any questions you are struggling with?"

3 Briefly explain the answer to any questions they might have, referring back to the specific page in the workbook.

When we choose not to forgive, we turn our backs on God and the-best-version-of-ourselves. Everybody needs to forgive somebody. Whom is God inviting you to forgive?

Rediscover Jesus

Show What You Know

True or False

1. __F__ Ordinary moments can never be great. (p 139)

2. __T__ Your First Reconciliation is one of the great moments in your life. (p 139)

3. __F__ It is never good to prepare for the important moments in your life. (p 144)

4. __F__ God wants us to be restless and unhappy. (p 149)

5. __T__ God's love is greater than any sin you could ever commit. (p 165)

Fill in the blank

1. God is the best _____friend_____ you will ever have. (p 168)

2. Following your conscience makes you _____happy_____ and ignoring your conscience makes you _____unhappy_____. (p 148)

3. You _____confess_____ your sins to the priest. (p 154)

4. Penance is like _____exercise_____ for the soul to help it get healthy again. (p 156)

5. Our Savior _____Jesus_____ suffered and died for us. (p 158)

My Notes:

_____

_____

_____

_____

_____

_____

_____

6. _____**Preparation**_____ is essential for a great experience. (p 144)

7. Confessing your sins through a priest to _____**God**_____ is a beautiful way to grow spiritually. (p 155)

8. God's _____**grace**_____ empowers you to make better choices in life. (p 161)

9. God blesses you with a _____**conscience**_____ to help you become the-best-version-of-yourself and live a holy life. (p 148)

10. God will never stop _____**encouraging**_____ you to become the-best-version-of-yourself, grow in virtue, and live a holy life. (p 167)

Word Bank

ENCOURAGING	CONFESS	HAPPY	PREPARATION	UNHAPPY
GRACE	CONSCIENCE	EXERCISE	JESUS	GOD	FRIEND

10 minutes

There is always a danger that we may just do the work for the sake of the work. This is where the respect and the love and the devotion come in—that we do it to God, to Christ, and that's why we try to do it as beautifully as possible.

St. Teresa of Calcutta

JOURNAL WITH JESUS

Step-by-Step

1 Invite your children to write a letter to Jesus.

2 Ask the children to remain silent during their journaling time.

3 You may wish to play some quiet, reflective music to help create the right mood in the classroom and to encourage the students to remain quiet and focused on journaling with Jesus.

Jesus wants you to be generous with your praise and encouragement. He wants you to be generous with your compassion and patience.

Rediscover Jesus

172

My Notes:

_____

_____

_____

_____

_____

_____

_____

_____

_____

Journal with Jesus

Dear Jesus,

When I think of you on the cross I am thankful because . . .

_____

_____

_____

_____

_____

_____

_____

_____

5 minutes

_____

_____

_____

_____

_____

_____

_____

tip

If we are not accustomed to this type of reflection, the journaling process can be difficult, even painful. But the rewards for doing this kind of work cannot be overstated. They reach into every aspect of our lives, by making us more aware of who we are and what we are here for.

It is only with gratitude that life becomes rich.

Dietrich Bonhoeffer

CLOSING PRAYER

Step-by-Step

1 Take a moment to gather the children and quiet them down in preparation for the closing prayer. Wait until they are settled and ready to pray.

2 Watch Episode 7.

3 Ask the children: What are some of the most important things you learned in this session?

- MY FIRST RECONCILIATION IS GOING TO BE A GREAT MOMENT IN MY LIFE.
- PREPARATION IS ESSENTIAL FOR A GREAT EXPERIENCE.
- THERE ARE FIVE STEPS TO A GREAT RECONCILIATION.
- GOD WILL REJOICE EVERY TIME WE COME TO RECONCILIATION.
- RECONCILIATION IS A LIFELONG BLESSING.
- GOD IS THE BEST FRIEND I WILL EVER HAVE.

Closing Prayer

One of the reasons God invites us to come to Reconciliation is so that we can continue to grow in virtue and happiness, so we can help him build his kingdom. God's kingdom is one of peace, love, and joy. He wants us to share this peace, love, and joy with everyone we meet.

But sometimes rather than humbly helping God build his kingdom, we become selfish and filled with pride and decide to build our own kingdom instead. Can you think of someone in history who focused on trying to build his or her own kingdom instead of helping God build his kingdom of peace, love, and joy?

To praise God and to remind ourselves that our mission is to help God build his kingdom and not get caught up in building our own selfish kingdoms, we pray a prayer called the Glory Be. It is a short but powerful prayer.

Let's all stand up and hold hands and pray it together:

> **Glory be to the Father,**
> **and to the Son,**
> **and to the Holy Spirit.**
> **As it was in the beginning,**
> **is now, and ever shall be,**
> **world without end.**
>
> **Amen.**

My Notes:

_____

_____

_____

_____

_____

_____

2 minutes

tip

Thank them for coming. Never stop thanking them for coming. Tell them you enjoyed your time with them. Talk about something during the class that made you think or laugh. Remind them you are praying for them.

The stillness of prayer is the most essential condition for fruitful action. Before all else, the disciple kneels down.

St. Gianna Molla

6

It's Only the Beginning

QUICK SESSION OVERVIEW

Opening Prayer. . . . . 5 min

Watch and Discuss; Read and Explore . . . . 65 min

Show What You Know . . . . 10 min

Journal with Jesus. . . . . 5 min

Closing Prayer. . . . . 5 min

OBJECTIVES

- **TO DEMONSTRATE** that great habits help us become the-best-version-of-ourselves.

- **TO EXPLAIN** that, daily prayer helps us hear God's voice and gives us courage to do what he is inviting us to do.

- **TO TEACH** that gratitude for God's blessings fills us with joy.

FIND YOUR PLACE IN GOD'S STORY,
REMEMBERING HE WANTS YOU TO BECOME . . .

• **The-best-version-of-yourself.**

• **A saint.**

① WELCOME

Are you ready for your students? Are they driving you crazy? Have you had a tough day?

Here is something to remember: When people have questions about the faith, those questions are beautiful because they represent a person's deepest yearnings. It doesn't matter how aggressively or disrespectfully the questions are asked. Never forget that every question comes from a yearning to know, love, and serve God. Young people may come at it in a very roundabout way, but don't we all?

Finally, throughout all of this, keep in mind that some of these children have already been hurt in ways we could not have imagined at their age. So love them and be patient and gentle with them. As Venerable Fulton Sheen once wrote: "Patience is power. Patience is not an absence of action; rather it is 'timing.' It waits on the right time to act, for the right reasons, and in the right way."

**Prayer
Icon**

**Read and
Explore**

**Watch and
Discuss**

**Show What
You Know**

**Journal
with Jesus**

**Time
Tracker**

OPENING PRAYER

Step-by-Step

1 Get them quiet. If you can't get your children quiet at the beginning of the class, the chances of you having control throughout rapidly diminish. Make sure they know that you are in charge. That doesn't mean you need to shout at them, but be firm.

2 Pray the opening prayer.

Prayer transforms everything we do into excellence.

Mustard Seeds

My Notes:

_____

_____

_____

_____

_____

_____

_____

6

It's Only the Beginning

God, our loving Father,
thank you for all the ways you bless me.
Help me to be aware that every person,
place, and adventure I experience is an
opportunity to love you more.
Fill me with a desire to change and to grow,
and give me the wisdom to choose
the-best-version-of-myself in
every moment of every day.

Amen.

5 minutes

tip
Thank the children for coming. Tell them you are happy to see them. This is the last class before they make their First Reconciliation. Ask them how they feel about it. Are they nervous? Excited? Both? Don't try and solve anything or change how they feel; simply listen. Make them feel heard. Thank them for sharing how they feel, and allow this session to be the last bit of encouragement they need.

If the children have already received their First Reconciliation prior to the class, ask them how it went. When they are finished sharing, encourage them to make regular Reconciliation a lifelong habit.

Prayer is the best weapon we have; it is the key to God's heart. You must speak to Jesus not only with your lips, but with your heart.

St. Pio of Pietrelcina

177

WATCH AND DISCUSS

Step-by-Step

1 Introduce the first episode by saying: "This episode is all about great moments. Can you think of a great moment in your life so far?"

2 Watch Episode 1.

3 Have the children share a great moment in their lives: a favorite birthday, the first goal in soccer, a new pet, etc. Then, share with the children why you're excited for them to make their First Reconciliation.

Grace is the help God gives us to respond to his call, and to do what is good and right.

Decision Point

178

My Notes:

_____
_____
_____
_____
_____
_____
_____

So Much to Look Forward To

We are so blessed to have God as our Father. We are so blessed to have Jesus as our friend and Savior. We are so blessed to have the Holy Spirit to lead and guide us.

Remember, God wants you to become the-best-version-of-yourself, grow in virtue, and live a holy life.

He gives us his grace through great moments like Baptism, First Reconciliation, First Communion, and Confirmation. But when we go to Mass on Sunday and spend a few minutes each day praying, he also gives us the grace we need to thrive every day.

🕐 **10 minutes**

tip

Statistics show that active listeners retain far more information than passive listeners. Here are two simple ways to encourage the children to be active listeners:

- *Describe each episode briefly before watching. New information can often be hard to process. Context gives children key points to focus on and a frame of reference, which makes the information much easier to grasp.*

- *Ask them a question before the episode starts. That way, as the episode progresses, they will be actively looking for the answer.*

When we teach children to be good, to be gentle, to be forgiving, to be generous, to love their fellow men, to regard this present age as nothing, we instill virtue in their souls, and reveal the image of God within them.

St. John Chrysostom

179

WATCH AND DISCUSS

Step-by-Step

1 Introduce Episode 2 by asking: "Did you know that God speaks to us? In this episode Fr. Tom and Ben have a great conversation about all the ways we can hear God's voice in our lives.

2 Watch Episode 2.

> **God wants you to live an excellent life. In that quest for excellence you will find rare happiness.**
>
> Resisting Happiness

The Will of God and Happiness

Prayer also helps us to discover God's will for our lives. It is by doing his will that we become the-best-version-of-ourselves and live holy lives. As we grow in wisdom we also discover that we are happiest when we are trying to do God's will, because it leads to happiness in this life and happiness for eternity with God in heaven.

Is it difficult to know God's will? Sometimes it is. But most of the time we know what God wants us to do.

My Notes:

_____

_____

_____

_____

_____

_____

_____

God wants us to make good choices
and avoid bad choices.

God wants us to do things that are good
and avoid things that are bad.

God wants us to be a good son or daughter,
and God wants us to be a good friend.

For the most part you already know what God's will is. But every day he talks to us all in different ways to help us know his will more clearly.

5 minutes

Prayer is the place of refuge for every worry, a foundation for cheerfulness, a source of constant happiness, a protection against sadness.

St. John Chrysostom

WATCH AND DISCUSS

Step-by-Step

1 Introduce Episode 3 by asking them: "Has anyone ever really taught you how to pray?" Share with the children how you learned to pray and how you wish you could have had access to an episode like the one they are about to watch when you were their age.

2 Watch Episode 3.

If you want to be happy, if you want to be calm and peaceful, if you want your life to be filled with joy: pray.

Mustard Seeds

The Prayer Process

God loves it when we talk to him. He loves it when we talk to him in our hearts throughout the day. He also loves it when we take a few minutes each day just to talk to him.

We call this conversation with God prayer. Sometimes when we sit down to pray we don't know what to say to him. The Prayer Process is a simple way to make sure we always have something to say to God. It is made up of seven easy steps. Each step is designed to guide your daily conversation with God.

My Notes:

_____

_____

_____

_____

_____

_____

1. Thank God for whoever and whatever you are most grateful for today.

2. Think about yesterday. Talk to God about the times when you were and were not the-best-version-of-yourself.

3. What do you think God is trying to say to you today? Talk to him about that.

4. Ask God to forgive you for anything you have done wrong and to fill your heart with peace.

5. Talk to God about some way he is inviting you to change and grow.

6. Pray for the other people in your life by asking God to guide them and watch over them.

7. Pray the Our Father.

This is a simple way to have a conversation with God each day during your quiet time. Through prayer God helps us to become the-best-version-of-ourselves, grow in virtue, and live holy lives.

10 minutes

tip

There are two problems that prevent Christians from developing a daily habit of prayer. The first is that most people have never been taught how to pray. The second is that when people do make a sincere effort to pray, they don't know where to start or finish or what to do, so they tend to sit down and just see what happens. The Prayer Process was developed to give people a format for their daily prayer experience. It has a starting point and an ending point. It is a simple way to focus our prayer time and facilitate an intimate conversation with God. If used daily, the Prayer Process will help these children to hear God's voice and discern his will for their lives.

Spiritual joy arises from the purity of heart and perseverance in prayer.

St. Francis of Assisi

WATCH AND DISCUSS

Step-by-Step

1 Activity: HIDE AND SEEK
Take a Prayer Process card and show it to the children. Tell them you are going to hide it somewhere in the room. Then, have the children cover their eyes with their hands or on their desks. While the children can't see, hide the card somewhere in the room. Once it's hidden, tell the children they can open their eyes. Give them two minutes to find the Prayer Process card. If they haven't found it after two minutes, provide hints so that the card can be found quickly.

2 Get the children settled down and back in their seats. Introduce the next episode by saying: "Great habits help us to become the-best-version-of-our-selves. In this episode Ben, Sarah, Hemingway, and their friends share with us some of their favorite habits."

3 Watch Episode 4.

The Power of Great Habits

Habits play a very important role in our lives. There are good habits and bad habits. Good habits help us become the-best-version-of-ourselves. Bad habits stop us from becoming all God created us to be.

Your parents, teachers, and coaches are all working very hard to help you develop good habits. Here are some examples of good habits:

- Drinking lots of water
- Eating fruits and vegetables
- Reading every day
- Spending time with friends
- Encouraging the people around you
- Going to church on Sunday
- Praying for a few minutes every day

My Notes:

_____

_____

_____

_____

_____

_____

Here are some examples of bad habits:

- Watching too much TV

- Eating too much junk food

- Not taking care of your things

- Bullying other children

- Missing Mass on Sunday

10 minutes

tip

Consider dimming the lights or turning them off before watching an episode of the animation. The dulling of lights creates a level of calmness and quiet in the classroom. It also proves to focus children's attention on what they are about to watch. If they are struggling to focus or are still animated after the activity, dimming the lights will help get the class refocused on what's next.

Let us not become weary in doing good, for at the proper time we will reap the harvest if we do not give up.

Galatians 6:9

READ AND EXPLORE

Step-by-Step

1 Read aloud the section on daily prayer.

2 Is there someone in history you really admire? If so, share with the children a little bit about this person, why you admire him or her, and how he or she became a great champion. You could talk about a great leader like Abraham Lincoln, a great athlete like Michael Jordan, a great musician like Mozart, a great artist like Picasso, or a great saint like Francis. No matter whom you choose, encourage the children to see the connection between great champions and great habits.

Youthfulness is not about being young; it is about allowing courage to rule over fear; it's about enthusiasm.

Mustard Seeds

Daily Prayer

The champions of every sport become great champions by having great habits. They practice hard and eat healthy foods. The champions of our faith became saints by having great habits. They practiced being patient and kind, generous and compassionate—and they prayed every day.

The habit of daily prayer will help you discover the voice of God in your life and give you the courage to do what God is inviting you to do.

My Notes:

_____

_____

_____

_____

_____

_____

_____

The Prayer Process is a great habit that will help you to become the-best-version-of-yourself and live a holy life.

We find incredible happiness in doing God's will. By spending a few minutes in quiet prayer each day and going to Mass each Sunday you will discover God's will for your life.

You are blessed. The more you embrace the habit of daily prayer, the more blessed you will become.

5 minutes

tip

If you are following the suggested 90-minute format, this marks the approximate halfway point. It is a good time for a brief break. If you are running behind, take a quick look ahead and see where you can get back on track. If ahead of schedule, look for an opportunity in the next 45 minutes to spark a great conversation. If on time, press on and finish strong!

Be patient with everyone, but above all with yourself. Do not be disheartened by your imperfections, but always rise up with fresh courage.

St. Francis de Sales.

WATCH AND DISCUSS

Step-by-Step

1 Introduce the next episode by asking: "Who's ready to learn one of Jesus' favorite habits?"

2 Watch Episode 5.

3 After the episode ask: "If Jesus needed quiet time, don't you think we do too?"

Silence and solitude give a perspective to the situations of our lives that could not be gained by a thousand hours of conversation or a thousand pages of books.

The Rhythm of Life

From the Bible: Jesus Went to a Quiet Place

One day Jesus was having dinner at a friend's house. When the people in the village heard that Jesus was there, they brought their sick friends and relatives to him and asked him to heal them. He healed the sick and the people were amazed. Very early the next morning Jesus went off alone and found a quiet place so he could pray.

My Notes:

_____

_____

_____

_____

_____

_____

_____

This is only one of many times in the Bible when we read about Jesus going off to a quiet place to pray. We all need a few minutes each day in a quiet place to sit and talk with God.

One of the best habits you can develop in life is the habit of daily prayer.

Sometimes when you sit down to spend some quiet time with God in prayer you don't know what to say. So, to help you with that, we have taught you the Prayer Process to guide your daily conversation with God.

If Jesus needed quiet time, don't you think we do too?

8 minutes

tip

In the episode, Ben and Sarah share where they go to spend 10 minutes in the classroom of silence every day. Help the children brainstorm some ideas of where they could spend their 10 minutes of quiet time with Jesus. Try to make sure they choose a place they can go each day and be alone.

Let all that I am wait quietly before God, for my hope is in him.

Psalm 62:5

WATCH AND DISCUSS

Step-by-Step

1 Introduce the next episode by saying: "In this episode, Tiny is feeling very sad but Ben, Sarah, and Hemingway suggest an activity to help Tiny remember how blessed he is."

2 Watch Episode 6.

Every relationship improves when we really start to listen, especially our relationship with God.

Resisting Happiness

190

Be Grateful

The best way to begin each day is by being grateful. Thanking God for another day is a simple way to talk to him as we get out of bed each morning.

Being grateful is also the best way to begin our daily prayer—that's why the first step in the Prayer Process is about GRATITUDE.

My Notes:

_____

_____

_____

_____

_____

_____

_____

By taking time to reflect on all the ways God has blessed us we become filled with gratitude and God fills us with joy. So anytime you are sad or feeling a little down, talk to God about everyone and everything you are grateful for.

It might help to make a gratitude list. Some people make a gratitude list and carry it around with them everywhere they go, in their pocket, wallet, or purse. Then if something bad happens or they are feeling a little down, they take out their gratitude list and pray through it.

Let's make our very own gratitude list together now.

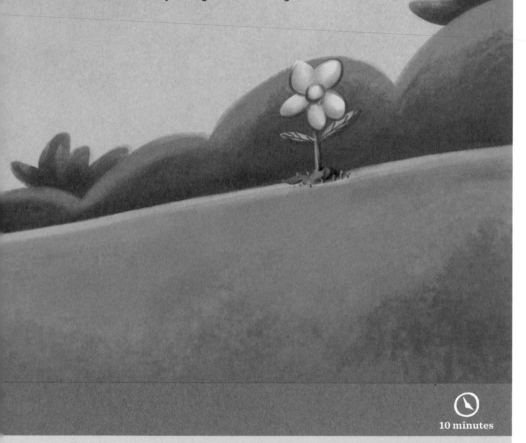

🕐
10 minutes

tip

Remember, repetition is critical to retaining information. After you watch the episode, have one of the children read the first paragraph out loud. Then ask, "So, what is the best way to begin each day?" Ask over and over again until the class responds emphatically: "With gratitude!" Beginning every day by thanking God may sound like a small thing, but imagine if every child in the room started doing this daily. It would be an absolute game changer.

To be grateful is to recognize the love of God in everything he has given us— and he has given us everything.

Thomas Merton

READ AND EXPLORE

Step-by-Step

1. Give the children 5 minutes to make their own gratitude list. If you don't have time, ask the children to make their list at home.

We must each learn to trust that we are here for a reason and that, no doubt, whether we are aware of it or not, things are unfolding just as they should be.

Rhythm of Life

My Notes:

_____
_____
_____
_____
_____
_____
_____
_____

I am grateful for . . .

_____

_____

_____

_____

_____

_____

_____

5 minutes

_____
_____
_____
_____
_____
_____
_____
_____

Give yourself fully to God. He will use you to accomplish great things on the condition that you believe much more in his love than in your own weakness.

St. Teresa of Calcutta

Step-by-Step

1. Congratulate the children on making their First Reconciliation!

2. Let them know how excited you are for them to experience their next Catholic Moment: First Communion.

Live joyfully and generously, with the kindness of the saints, trusting always in God, who loves you and wants good things for you.

Decision Point

God Fills You With Joy

Throughout your life there are going to be many wonderful things that happen. There are also going to be days when things happen that get you down a bit. Whether you are having a great day or a not-so-good day, it's always a good idea to spend a few minutes talking to God about all you are grateful for. We praise God by being grateful, and he responds by filling us with joy.

My Notes:

_____

_____

_____

_____

_____

_____

_____

Congratulations!

Congratulations on making your First Reconciliation. This is a wonderful time in your life. You are blessed.

The next great Catholic Moment in your journey will be your First Communion.

We hope the lessons you have learned in preparing for your First Reconciliation will live in your heart forever. We hope they will help you become the-best-version-of-yourself, grow in virtue, and live a holy life. We hope they will help you to never forget that YOU ARE BLESSED!

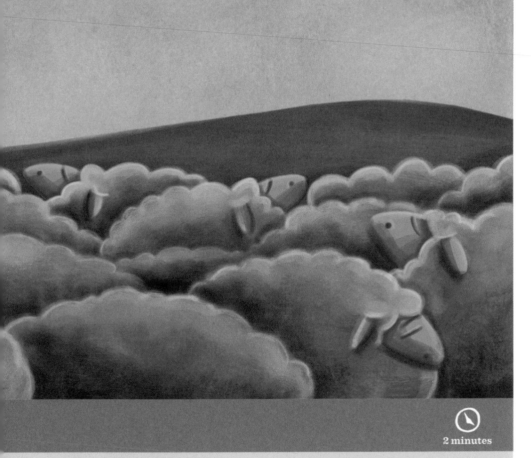

2 minutes

tip

Thank them for making this journey with you. Tell them you have enjoyed your time with them. Talk about the highlights of your time together. Funny moments. Serious moments. Life-changing moments.

Remind them you will be praying for them for the rest of their lives. Encourage them to explore their faith. Promise them that the day will come when they will be glad they took this stuff seriously.

The end for which we were created invites us to walk a road that is surely sown with a lot of thorns, but it is not sad; through even the sorrow, it is illuminated by joy.

Blessed Pierre Giorgio Frassati

195

Step-by-Step

1 Have your children complete the activity page by themselves, with a partner, or as a group.

2 After three minutes ask the class: "Are there any questions you are struggling with?"

3 Briefly explain the answer to any questions they might have, referring back to the specific page in the workbook.

God has a plan for his children. But he needs your help to fulfill his plan.

Decision Point

Show What You Know

True or False

1. __T__ You are blessed to have God as your Father. (p 179)

2. __T__ Prayer helps you discover God's will for your life. (p 180)

3. __F__ Jesus always went to a loud place to speak with God. (p 188)

4. __T__ God wants to tell you something every time you go to Mass. (p 187)

5. __T__ Gratitude fills us with joy. (p 191)

Fill in the blank

1. Doing God's will leads to happiness in this life and ___**happiness**___ for eternity with God in heaven. (p 180)

2. God wants to ___**bless**___ you in a thousand different ways so you can live a fabulous life. (p 179)

3. It is by doing God's will that you become the ___**the-best-version-of-yourself**___. (p 180)

4. The more you embrace the habit of daily ___**prayer**___ (p 186) the more blessed you will become.

5. As you grow in ___**wisdom**___ you will discover that you are happiest when you are trying to do God's will. (p 187)

My Notes:

_____

_____

_____

_____

_____

_____

_____

6. God wants us to do things that are _____**good**_____ and avoid _____**bad**_____ choices. (p 184)

7. Jesus is your _____**friend**_____ and _____**Savior**_____. (p 179)

8. One great way to have a daily conversation with God is by using the _____**Prayer Process**_____. (p 182)

9. The champions of our Catholic faith become saints by having great _____**habits**_____. (p 184)

10. The best way to begin each day is by being _____**grateful**_____. (p 190)

Word Bank

BLESS   GOOD   BAD   HABITS   WISDOM   SAVIOR   PRAYER   FRIEND

THE-BEST-VERSION-OF-YOURSELF   PRAYER PROCESS   HAPPINESS   GRATEFUL

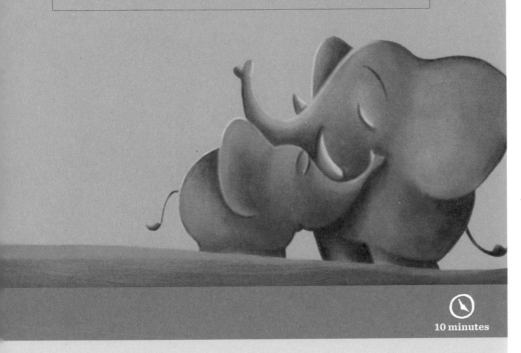

🕐 **10 minutes**

_____

_____

_____

_____

_____

_____

tip

Even though it's the last session, completing the Show What You Know section is still as important as it was the first time you met. This is a great time to reinforce some of the most important themes covered during the First Reconciliation experience. Don't let this opportunity get away from you.

Great occasions for serving God come seldom, but little ones surround us daily.

St. Francis de Sales

JOURNAL WITH JESUS

Step-by-Step

1. Invite your children to write a letter to Jesus.

2. Ask the children to remain silent during their journaling time.

3. You may wish to play some quiet, reflective music to help create the right mood in the classroom and to encourage the students to remain quiet and focused on journaling with Jesus.

Allow the love that flows to you from God to flow out of you to others.

Decision Point

My Notes:

_____
_____
_____
_____
_____
_____
_____
_____

Journal with Jesus

Dear Jesus,

I am so blessed to have had my First Reconciliation because . . .

_____

_____

_____

_____

_____

_____

_____

🕐
5 minutes

_____

_____

_____

_____

_____

_____

_____

If you are what you could be you would set the world ablaze!

St. Catherine of Siena

CLOSING PRAYER

Step-by-Step

1 Take a moment to gather the children and quiet them down in preparation for the closing prayer. Wait until they are settled and ready to pray.

2 Watch Episode 7.

3 Ask the children: "What are some of the most important things you learned in this session?"

- I AM BLESSED.
- PRAYER HELPS US DISCOVER GOD'S WILL FOR OUR LIVES.
- GREAT HABITS HELP US BECOME THE-BEST-VERSION-OF-OURSELVES.
- BEING GRATEFUL MEANS THANKING GOD FOR ALL THE WAYS HE HAS BLESSED ME.
- GOD WANTS ME TO BE HAPPY.

Closing Prayer

Saint Francis of Assisi lived in Italy about 800 years ago. He loved God very much and dedicated his life to teaching people about Jesus. This beautiful prayer of St. Francis was written to help us put things in perspective. It is so easy to get confused about what matters most. Prayer helps us get our priorities straight. Let's pray Saint Francis' prayer together:

My Notes:

_____
_____
_____
_____
_____
_____
_____
_____

Lord, make me an instrument of your peace:
where there is hatred, let me sow love;
where there is injury, pardon;
where there is doubt, faith;
where there is despair, hope;
where there is darkness, light;
where there is sadness, joy.

O Divine Master, grant that I may not so much seek
to be consoled as to console,
to be understood as to understand,
to be loved as to love.
For it is in giving that we receive,
it is in pardoning that we are pardoned,
and it is in dying that we are born to eternal life.

Amen.

5 minutes

Consult not your fears but your hopes and your dreams. Think not about your frustrations, but about your unfulfilled potential. Concern yourself not with what you tried and failed in, but with what it is still possible for you to do.

St. John XXIII

My Little Catechism

Your fabulous journey with God is just beginning. Along the way you will have many questions. Questions are good. God places questions in your heart and mind for many different reasons. Follow your questions, wherever they might lead you.

Some of your questions will be easy to find answers to. To help us answer many of our questions, our spiritual leaders have given us the Catechism of the Catholic Church. The answers we find there have been revealed by God and by nature over the centuries.

In the pages that follow we will share with you some questions you may have about God and life. The answers are easy to read but often hard to live. But the answers will help you become the-best-version-of-yourself, grow in virtue, and live a holy life.

There will be other times in your life when you have questions that cannot be answered by words on a page, for example what Vocation you are called to or what career you should pursue. At these times you will seek deeply personal answers to deeply personal questions.

These questions require a lot more patience. Seek the advice of wise people who love the Lord. Read what wise men and women before you have had to say on such topics. But, most of all, pray and ask God to show you his way.

As you make this journey you will encounter others who have questions. Help them as best you can to find the answers. People deserve answers to their questions.

And never, ever, forget . . . you are blessed!

1. **Q: Who made you?**

   A: God made you.

   > In the Bible: Genesis 1:1, 26–27; Genesis 2:7, 21–22
   > In the Catechism: CCC 355

2. **Q: Does God love you?**

   A: Yes. God loves you more than anyone in the world,
   and more than you could ever imagine.

   > In the Bible: John 3:16
   > In the Catechism: CCC 457, 458

3. **Q: Why did God make you?**

   A: God made you to know him, love him, to carry out the mission he entrusts to
   you in this world, and to be happy with Him forever in Heaven.

   > In the Bible: Deuteronomy 10:12–15; John 17:3
   > In the Catechism: CCC 1, 358

4. **Q: What is God?**

   A: God is an infinite and perfect spirit.

   > In the Bible: Exodus 3:6; Isaiah 44:6; 1 John 4:8, 16
   > In the Catechism: CCC 198–200, 212, 221

5. **Q: Did God have a beginning?**

   A: No. God has no beginning. He always was and he always will be.

   > In the Bible: Psalm 90:2; Revelation 1:8
   > In the Catechism: CCC 202

6. **Q: Where is God?**

   A: Everywhere

   > In the Bible: Psalm 139
   > In the Catechism: CCC 1

7. **Q: Does God see us?**

   A: God sees us and watches over us.

   > In the Bible: Wisdom 11:24–26; Jeremiah 1:5
   > In the Catechism: CCC 37, 301, 302

8. **Q: Does God know everything?**

   A: Yes. God knows all things, even our most secret thoughts, words, and actions.

   > In the Bible: Job 21:22; Psalm 33:13–15; Psalm 147:4–5
   > In the Catechism: CCC 208

9. **Q: Is God all loving, just, holy, and merciful?**

   A: Yes, God is loving, all just, all holy, and all merciful—and he invites us to be loving, just, holy, and merciful too.

   > In the Bible: John 13:34; 1 John 4:8; Ephesians 2:4
   > In the Catechism: CCC 214, 211, 208

10. **Q: Is there only one God?**

    A: Yes, there is only one God.

    > In the Bible: Isaiah 44:6; John 8:58
    > In the Catechism: CCC 253

11. **Q: Why is there only one God?**

    A: There can only be one God, because God, being supreme and infinite, cannot have an equal.

    > In the Bible: Mark 12:29–30
    > In the Catechism: CCC 202

12. **Q: How many Persons are there in God?**

    A: In God there are three Divine Persons, unique and distinct and yet equal in all things—the Father, the Son, and the Holy Spirit.

    > In the Bible: 1 Corinthians 12:4–6; 2 Corinthians 13:13; Ephesians 4:4–6
    > In the Catechism: CCC 252, 254, 255

13. **Q: Is the Father God?**

    A: Yes.

    > In the Bible: Exodus 3:6; Exodus 4:22
    > In the Catechism: CCC 253, 262

14. **Q: Is the Son God?**

    A: Yes.

    > In the Bible: John 8:58; John 10:30
    > In the Catechism: CCC 253, 262

15. **Q: Is the Holy Spirit God?**

A: Yes.

> In the Bible: John 14:26; John 15:26
> In the Catechism: CCC 253, 263

16. **Q: What is the Holy Trinity?**

A: The Holy Trinity is one God in three divine persons—Father, Son, and Holy Spirit.

> In the Bible: Matthew 28:19
> In the Catechism CCC 249, 251

17. **Q. What is free will?**

A: Free will is an incredible gift from God that allows us to make our own decisions. This incredible gift comes with incredible responsibility.

> In the Bible: Sirach 15:14–15
> In the Catechism: CCC 1731

18. **Q. What is sin?**

A: Sin is any willful thought, word, deed, or omission contrary to the law of God.

> In the Bible: Genesis 3:5; Exodus 20:1–17
> In the Catechism: CCC 1850

19. **Q: How many kinds of sin are there?**

A: There are two actual kinds of sin—venial and mortal.

> In the Bible: 1 John 5:16–17
> In the Catechism: CCC 1855

20. **Q: What is a venial sin?**

A: Venial is a slight offense against God.

> In the Bible: Matthew 5:19; Matthew 12:32; 1 John 5:16–18
> In the Catechism: CCC 1855, 1863

21. **Q: What is a mortal sin?**

A: Mortal sin is a grievous offense against God and his law.

> In the Bible: Matthew 12:32; 1 John 5:16–18
> In the Catechism: CCC 1855, 1857

22. **Q: Does God abandon us when we sin?**

A: Never. God is always calling to us, pleading with us, to return to him and his ways.

In the Bible: Psalm 103: 9–10, 13; Jeremiah 3:22; Matthew 28:20; Luke 15:11-32
In the Catechism: CCC 27, 55, 982

23. **Q: Which Person of the Holy Trinity became man?**

A: The Second Person, God the Son, became man without giving up his divine nature.

In the Bible: 1 John 4:2
In the Catechism: CCC 423, 464

24. **Q: What name was given to the Second Person of the Holy Trinity when he became man?**

A: Jesus.

In the Bible: Luke 1:31; Matthew 1:21
In the Catechism: CCC 430

25. **Q: When the Son became man, did he have a human mother?**

A: Yes.

In the Bible: Luke 1:26–27
In the Catechism: CCC 488, 490, 495

26. **Q: Who was Jesus' mother?**

A: The Blessed Virgin Mary.

In the Bible: Luke 1:30, 31; Matthew 1:21–23
In the Catechism: CCC 488, 495

27. **Q: Why do we honor Mary?**

A: Because she is the mother of Jesus and our mother too.

In the Bible: Luke 1:48; John 19:27
In the Catechism: CCC 971

28. **Q: Who was Jesus' real father?**

A: God the Father.

In the Bible: Luke 1:35; John 17:1
In the Catechism CCC 422, 426, 442

29. **Q: Who was Jesus' foster father?**

A: Joseph.

> In the Bible: Matthew 1:19, 20; Matthew 2:13, 19–21
> In the Catechism: CCC 437, 488, 1655

30. **Q: Is Jesus God, or is he man, or is he both God and man?**

A: Jesus is both God and man; as the Second Person of the Holy Trinity, he is God; and since he took on a human nature from his mother Mary, he is man.

> In the Bible: Philippians 2: 6–7; John 1:14, 16; John 13:3; 1 John 4:2
> In the Catechism: CCC 464, 469

31. **Q: Was Jesus also a man?**

A: Yes, Jesus was fully God and fully human.

> In the Bible: Luke 24:39; 1 John 4:2–3
> In the Catechism: CCC 464, 469, 470

32. **Q: On what day was Jesus born?**

A: Jesus was born on Christmas day in a stable in Bethlehem.

> In the Bible: Luke 2:1–20; Matthew 1:18–25
> In the Catechism: CCC 437, 563

33. **Q: What is the Incarnation?**

A: The Incarnation is the belief that Jesus became man.

> In the Bible: John 1:14; 1 John 4:2
> In the Catechism: CCC 461, 463

34. **Q: Did Jesus love life?**

A: Yes.

> In the Bible: John 10:10; John 2:1–12
> In the Catechism: CCC 221, 257, 989

35. **Q: If Jesus loved life why did he willingly die on the cross?**

A: He died on the cross because he loved you and me even more than life.

> In the Bible: Romans 5:8; John 15:13; Ephesians 5:2
> In the Catechism: CCC 1825, 604

36. Q: Why did Jesus suffer and die?

A: So that we could be forgiven our sins, and live with him in heaven forever after this life.

In the Bible: John 3:16; 2 Corinthians 5:14–16
In the Catechism: CCC 604, 618, 620

37. Q: What do we call the mystery of God becoming man?

A: The mystery of the Incarnation.

In the Bible: John 1:14; 1 John 4:2
In the Catechism: CCC 461, 463

38. Q: On what day did Jesus die on the cross?

A: Good Friday, the day after the Last Supper.

In the Bible: John 19:16–40; Matthew 27:33–50
In the Catechism CCC 641

39. Q: On what day did Jesus rise from the dead?

A: On Easter Sunday, three days after Good Friday.

In the Bible: Matthew 28:1–6; Mark 16:1–8
In the Catechism: CCC 1169, 1170

40. Q: What gifts do we receive as a result of being saved by Jesus?

A: By dying on the cross Jesus restored our relationship with God and opened a floodgate of grace.

In the Bible: Luke 23:44–46; Romans 3:21–26; 2 Corinthians 5:17–21
In the Catechism: CCC 1026, 1047

41. Q: What is grace?

A: Grace is the help God gives us to respond generously to his call, to do what is good and right, grow in virtue, and live holy lives.

In the Bible: John 1:12–18; 2 Corinthians 12:9
In the Catechism: CCC 1996

42. Q: What is Faith?

A: Faith is a gift from God. It is a supernatural virtue that allows us to firmly believe all the truth that God has revealed to us.

In the Bible: Hebrews 11:1
In the Catechism: CCC 1814

43. **Q: What is Hope?**

A: Hope is a gift from God. It is a supernatural virtue that allows us to firmly trust that God will keep all his promises and lead us to heaven.

In the Bible: Romans 8:24–25; 1 Timothy 4:10; 1 Timothy 1:1; Hebrews 6:18–20
In the Catechism: CCC 1817, 1820–1821

44. **Q: What is Charity?**

A: Charity is a gift from God. It is a supernatural virtue that allows us to love God above everything else, and our neighbor as ourselves.

In the Bible: John 13:34; 1 Corinthians 13:4–13
In the Catechism: CCC 1822, 1823, 1825

45. **Q: Will God give you the gifts of Faith, Hope, and Charity?**

A: Yes, God gives the gifts of Faith, Hope, and Charity, freely to all those who ask for them sincerely and consistently.

In the Bible: 1 Corinthians 13:13
In the Catechism: 1813

46. **Q: How long will God love me for?**

A: God will love you forever.

In the Bible: John 13:1; Romans 8:35–39
In the Catechism: CCC 219

47. **Q: When did Jesus ascend into heaven?**

A: On Ascension Thursday, forty days after Easter.

In the Bible: Acts 1:9; Mark 16:19
In the Catechism: CCC 659

48. **Q: When did the Holy Spirit descend upon the Apostles?**

A: On Pentecost Sunday, fifty days after Easter.

In the Bible: John 20:21–22; Matthew 28:19
In the Catechism: CCC 731, 1302

49. **Q: What is meant by the Redemption?**

A: Redemption means that Jesus' Incarnation, life, death, and Resurrection paid the price for our sins, opened the gates of heaven, and freed us from slavery to sin and death.

In the Bible: Ephesians 1:7; Romans 4:25
In the Catechism CCC 517, 606, 613

50. **Q: What did Jesus establish to continue his mission of Redemption?**

A: He established the Catholic Church.

> In the Bible: Matthew 16:18
> In the Catechism: CCC 773, 778, 817, 822

51. **Q: Why do we believe that the Catholic Church is the one true Church?**

A: Because it is the only Church established by Jesus.

> In the Bible: Matthew 16:18
> In the Catechism: CCC 750

52. **Q: Does it matter to which Church or religion you belong?**

A: Yes, in order to be faithful to Jesus, it is necessary to remain in the Church he established.

> In the Bible: Mark 16:16; John 3:5
> In the Catechism: CCC 846

53. **Q: What are the Four Marks of the Church?**

A: One, Holy, Catholic, and Apostolic.

> In the Bible: Ephesians 2:20, 4:3, 5:26; Matthew 28:19; Revelation 21:14;
> In the Catechism: CCC 813, 823, 830, 857

54. **Q: How does the Church preserve the teachings of Jesus?**

A: Through Sacred Scripture and Sacred Tradition.

> In the Bible: 2 Timothy 2:2; 2 Thessalonians 2:15
> In the Catechism: CCC 78, 81, 82

55. **Q: How does the Church's calendar differ from the secular calendar?**

A: The first day of the Church's year is the first Sunday of Advent, not January 1st. The Church's calendar revolves around the life, death, and Resurrection of Jesus. Throughout the course of the Church's year the whole mystery of Jesus Christ is unfolded.

> In the Bible: Luke 2:1–20; 1 Corinthians 15:3–4
> In the Catechism: CCC 1163; 1171, 1194

Going Deeper

Over the course of the year, through the readings at Mass, the feast days and holy days, we experience the story of Jesus. The Church's calendar does this to remind us that Jesus' story is not just about what happened over two thousand years ago. It is about our friendship with him today. The mystery of his life, teachings, and saving grace are unfolding in your life and the life of the Church today.

56. Q: **Did Jesus give special authority to one of the Apostles?**
    A: Yes, to Peter when Jesus said to him, "I will give you the keys of the kingdom of heaven, and whatever you bind on earth shall be bound in heaven, and whatever you loose on earth shall be loosed in heaven."

    In the Bible: Mark 3:16, 9:2; Luke 24:34
    In the Catechism: CCC 552, 881

57. Q: **Who speaks with the authority that Jesus gave to St. Peter?**
    A: The pope who is St. Peter's successor, the Bishop of Rome, and the Vicar of Christ on earth.

    In the Bible: Matthew 16:18; John 21:15–17
    In the Catechism: CCC 891

58. Q: **What is the name of the present pope?**
    A: Pope Francis.

    In the Bible: Matthew 16:18; John 21:15–17
    In the Catechism: CCC 936

59. Q: **What is the sacred liturgy?**
    A: The Church's public worship of God.

    In the Bible: John 4:23–24
    In the Catechism: CCC 1069, 1070

60. Q: **What attitude should we have when we participate in the sacred liturgy?**
    A: We should have the attitude of reverence in our hearts and respect in our actions and appearance.

    In the Bible: Hebrews 12:28
    In the Catechism: CCC 2097

61. **Q: What is a Sacrament?**

A: A Sacrament is an outward sign, instituted by Christ and entrusted to the Church to give grace. Grace bears fruit in those who receive them with the required dispositions.

In the Bible: 2 Peter 1:4
In the Catechism: CCC 1131

Going Deeper

God gives you grace to help you do what is good and right. When you are open to God, he also gives you the grace to be kind, generous, courageous, and compassionate toward others. Grace bears good fruit in our lives. One of the most powerful ways God shares his grace with us is through the Sacraments. This grace helps us to become the-very-best-version-of-ourselves, grow in virtue, and live holy lives.

62. **Q: How does Jesus share his life with us?**

A: During his earthly life, Jesus shared his life with others through his words and actions; now he shares the very same life with us through the Sacraments.

In the Bible: John 3:16; John 6:5–7
In the Catechism: CCC 521; 1131, 1115–1116

Going Deeper

God loves to share his life and love with us. We can experience his life through daily prayer, Scripture, and through serving one another. The most powerful way that God shares his life with us is through the Sacraments. Sunday Mass and regular Reconciliation are two Sacraments that guide us and encourage us on our journey to become the-best-version-of-ourselves, grow in virtue, and live a holy life.

63. **Q: How many Sacraments are there?**

A: Seven.

In the Bible: John 20:22–23; Luke 22:14–20; John 7:37–39; James 5:14–16; Hebrews 5:1–6; Matthew 19:6
In the Catechism: CCC 1113

64. **Q: What are the Seven Sacraments; and which ones have you received?**

A: Baptism, Penance, Holy Eucharist, Confirmation, Holy Orders, Matrimony, Anointing of the Sick. You have received Baptism, Penance, and Holy Eucharist.

In the Bible: John 20:22–23; Luke 22:14–20; John 7:37–39; James 5:14–16; Hebrews 5:1–6; Matthew 19:6;
In the Catechism: CCC 1113

65. **Q: What are the Sacraments you can only receive once?**

A: Baptism, Confirmation, and Holy Orders.

> In the Bible: Ephesians 4:30
> In the Catechism: CCC 1272

66. **Q: How is Christian initiation accomplished?**

A: Christian initiation is accomplished with three Sacraments: Baptism which is the beginning of new life; Confirmation which strengthens our new life in Christ; and the Eucharist which nourishes the disciple with Jesus' Body and Blood so that we can be transformed in Christ.

> In the Bible: John 3:5; Acts 8:14–17; John 6:51–58
> In the Catechism: CCC 1212; 1275

Going Deeper

Life is a journey with God. Baptism, Confirmation and First Communion are all great moments in your journey. They are Sacraments that work together to help you live your best life. In Baptism you receive new life in Jesus, in Confirmation God reminds us that he has a special mission for each and every single one of us, and Holy Communion gives us the strength and the wisdom to live that mission by serving God and others.

67. **Q: When you were born, did you have Sanctifying Grace (a share in God's life)?**

A: No.

> In the Bible: Colossians 1:12–14
> In the Catechism: CCC 403, 1250

68. **Q: Why are we not born with Sanctifying Grace?**

A: Because we are born with original sin which is the loss of Sanctifying Grace.

> In the Bible: Genesis 3:23
> In the Catechism: CCC 403, 1250

69. **Q: Was any human person conceived without original sin?**

A: Yes, Mary at her Immaculate Conception.

> In the Bible: Luke 1:28
> In the Catechism: CCC 491, 492

70. **Q: What was the original sin?**

A: Adam and Eve were tempted by the devil; and they chose to distrust God's goodness and to disobey his law.

> In the Bible: Genesis 3:1–11; Romans 5:19
> In the Catechism: CCC 397

71. **Q: Is there really a devil?**

A: Yes.

> In the Bible: 1 John 5:19; 1 Peter 5:8
> In the Catechism: CCC 391

72. **Q: Is it easier to be bad or to be good?**

A: It is easier to be bad, because original sin has left us with an inclination to sin called concupiscence.

> In the Bible: Romans 7:15–18
> In the Catechism: CCC 409, 1264, 2516

73. **Q: When did you receive Sanctifying Grace for the first time?**

A: At Baptism.

> In the Bible: 2 Corinthians 5:17
> In the Catechism: CCC 1265

74. **Q: What is Baptism?**

A: Baptism is the Sacrament of rebirth in Jesus that is necessary for salvation.

> In the Bible: 2 Corinthians 5:17; 2 Peter 1:4; Galatians 4:5–7;
> In the Catechism: CCC 1266, 1277, 1279

Going Deeper

Baptism is a great blessing. Through your Baptism you became a member of the Catholic Church. This is another wonderful reason why being Catholic is a great blessing. Through your Baptism, you received new life in Jesus. You were made for mission. God had that mission in mind when you were baptized, and every day since he has been preparing you for your mission. We discover that mission through prayer, the Sacraments, and service to others. God doesn't reveal our mission all at once, he reveals it step-by-step.

75. **Q: What are the fruits of Baptism?**

A: Baptism makes us Christians, cleanses us of original sin and personal sin, and reminds us that we are children of God and members of the Body of Christ— the Church.

In the Bible: Galatians 4:5–7
In the Catechism: CCC 1279

Going Deeper

In Baptism God gives us many gifts. We become Christian, our sins are forgiven, we are given new life in Jesus, and God marks us for a great mission. God is able to do this through the power of the Holy Spirit. In Baptism our souls are flooded with the gift of the Holy Spirit, which helps us in our journey to grow closer to God. Each and every Sacrament we receive is full of gifts, big and small. Every blessing reminds us that we are all sons and daughters of a loving Father.

76. **Q: What did Baptism do for you?**

A: It gave me a share in God's life for the first time, made me a child of God, and took away original sin.

In the Bible: 2 Corinthians 5:17; 2 Peter 1:4; Galatians 4:5–7
In the Catechism: CCC 1266, 1279

77. **Q: How old does someone need to be to receive Baptism?**

A: A person can be baptized at any age. Since the earliest times of Christianity, Baptism has been administered to infant children because Baptism is a grace and a gift that is freely given by God and does not presuppose any human merit.

In the Bible: Acts 2:37–39
In the Catechism: CCC 1282

Going Deeper

God's love is a free gift. There is nothing you could do to earn or lose God's love. You may be tempted to think that God's love is something to be earned. This is simply not true. God loved you into life, and God loved you into the Church. You did nothing to be born, and if you were baptized as an infant you did nothing to be baptized. You didn't do anything to deserve life or Baptism. God freely gives you life and faith.

78. **Q: Who administers the Sacrament of Baptism?**

A: Anyone can administer the Sacrament of Baptism in an emergency by pouring water over that person's head and saying, "I baptize you in the name of the Father, and of the Son, and of the Holy Spirit." Baptism, however, is usually administered by a priest or deacon.

In the Bible: Matthew 28:19
In the Catechism: CCC 1284

Going Deeper

Not everyone is baptized as an infant. Some people don't learn about Jesus until they are adults. But God wants everyone to receive the blessing of Baptism. He wants everyone to be a part of his family—the Catholic Church. He wants everyone to be free from original sin. He wants everyone to have new life in his Son Jesus. He wants everyone to spend eternity with him in heaven.

79. **Q: How long do you remain a child of God?**

A: Forever.

In the Bible: 1 Peter 1:3—4
In the Catechism: CCC 1272, 1274

80. **Q: Can you lose a share in God's life after Baptism?**

A: Yes.

In the Bible: Mark 3:29
In the Catechism: CCC 1861

81. **Q: Can we lose the new life of grace that God has freely given us?**

A: Yes. The new life of grace can be lost by sin.

In the Bible:1 Corinthians 6:9; 2 Corinthians 5:19—21; 1 John 1:9
In the Catechism: CCC 1420

Going Deeper

At Baptism we are filled with a very special grace. This grace blesses us with new life and brings us into friendship with God. That new life can be hurt or lost when we sin. When that happens, don't worry because God has given us the blessing of Reconciliation! As long as we are truly sorry for our sins and go to Reconciliation, we can once again experience the fullness of life with God. Reconciliation is a great blessing!

82. **Q: How can you lose Sanctifying Grace (a share in God's life)?**

A: By committing mortal sin.

In the Bible: Galatians 5:19–21; Romans 1:28–32
In the Catechism: CCC 1861

83. **Q: What are the two kinds of personal sin (sin we commit ourselves)?**

A: Venial and mortal sin.

In the Bible: 1 John 5:16, 17
In the Catechism: CCC 1855

84. **Q: What is a venial Sin?**

A: Venial sin is a slight offense against God.

In the Bible: Matthew 5:19; Matthew 12:32; 1 John 5:16–18
In the Catechism: CCC 1855, 1863

85. **Q: What is a mortal sin?**

A: Mortal sin is a grievous offense against God and his law.

In the Bible: Matthew 12:32; 1 John 5:16–18
In the Catechism: CCC 1855, 1874

86. **Q: Does God abandon us when we sin?**

A: Never. God is always calling to us, pleading with us, to return to him and his ways.

In the Bible: Psalm 103:9–10, 13; Jeremiah 3:22; Matthew 28:20;
In the Catechism: CCC 55, 301, 410

87. **Q: Which is the worse sin?**

A: Mortal (deadly) sin.

In the Bible: 1 John 5:16
In the Catechism: CCC 1855, 1874, 1875

88. **Q: What three things are necessary to commit a mortal sin?**

A: 1. You must disobey God in a serious matter.

2. You must know that it is wrong.

3. You must freely choose to do it anyway.

In the Bible: Mark 10:19; Luke 16:19–31; James 2:10-11
In the Catechism: CCC 1857

89. **Q: What happens to you if you die in a state of mortal sin?**

A: You go to hell.

> In the Bible: 1 John 3:14–15; Matthew 25:41–46;
> In the Catechism: CCC 1035, 1472, 1861, 1874

90. **Q: Is there really a hell?**

A: Yes; it is the place of eternal separation from God.

> In the Bible: Isaiah 66:24; Mark 9:47, 48
> In the Catechism: CCC 1035

91. **Q: What happens if you die with venial sin on your soul?**

A: You go to purgatory where you are purified and made perfect.

> In the Bible: 1 Corinthians 3:14–15; 2 Maccabees 12:45–46
> In the Catechism: CCC 1030, 1031, 1472

92. **Q: What happens to the souls in purgatory after their purification?**

A: They go to heaven.

> In the Bible: 2 Maccabees 12:45
> In the Catechism: CCC 1030

93. **Q: Is there really a heaven?**

A: Yes; it is the place of eternal happiness with God.

> In the Bible: 1 John 3:2; 1 Corinthians 13:12; Revelation 22:4–5
> In the Catechism: CCC 1023, 1024

94. **Q: Can any sin, no matter how serious, be forgiven?**

A: Yes, any sin, no matter how serious or how many times it is committed can be forgiven.

> In the Bible: Matthew 18:21–22
> In the Catechism: CCC 982

95. **Q: What is the primary purpose of the Sacrament of Reconciliation?**

A: The primary purpose of the Sacrament of Reconciliation is the forgiveness of sins committed after Baptism.

> In the Bible: Sirach 18:12–13; Sirach 21:1; Acts 26:17–18
> In the Catechism: CCC 1421, 1446, 1468

Going Deeper

Through Baptism we become children of God, are welcomed into a life of grace, and given the promise of heaven. As we get older, we may do things that harm our relationship with God. But God keeps loving us, and invites us to participate in regular Reconciliation so that our friendship with him can always be as strong as it was in Baptism. If we offend God, the best thing to do is to say sorry to God by going to Reconciliation.

96. Q: What other names is the Sacrament of Reconciliation known by?

A: In different places and different times, the Sacrament of Reconciliation is also called the Sacrament of Conversion, Confession or Penance.

In the Bible: Mark 1:15; Proverbs 28:13; Acts 3:19; 2 Peter 3:9
In the Catechism: CCC 1423, 1424

Going Deeper

Jesus loves you and he wants to save you from your sins. He wants to save you because he wants to live in friendship with you on earth and in heaven. He wants to share his joy with you and he wants you to share that joy with others. No matter what name is used, the Sacrament of Reconciliation restores our friendship with God and helps us become the-best-version-of-ourselves, grow in virtue, and live a holy life.

97. Q: Is the Sacrament of Reconciliation a blessing?

A: Yes, it is a great blessing from God.

In the Bible: Psalm 32: 1–2; Romans 4:6–8
In the Catechism: CCC 1468, 1496

98. Q: Who commits sins?

A: All people sin.

In the Bible: Romans 3:23–25; 1 John 1:8–10
In the Catechism: CCC 827

99. Q: How can a mortal sin be forgiven?

A: Through the Sacrament of Reconciliation.

In the Bible: 2 Corinthians 5:20–21
In the Catechism: CCC 1446, 1497

100. **Q: What is the ordinary way for someone to be reconciled with God and his Church?**

A: The ordinary way for someone to be reconciled with God and his Church is by personally confessing all grave sin to a priest followed by absolution.

In the Bible: John 20:23
In the Catechism: CCC 1497

Going Deeper

We all stray away from God from time to time. When we do, it is a good time to go to the Sacrament of Reconciliation and say sorry to God. You might be tempted to fall into the trap of thinking that your sin is too big for God to forgive. But, there is nothing you can do that will make God stop loving you. The doors of the Church are always open and God is always willing to forgive us when are sorry. The Sacrament of Reconciliation is a great blessing!

101. **Q: What three things must you do in order to receive forgiveness of sin in the Sacrament of Confession?**

A: 1. You must be truly sorry for your sins.
2. Confess all mortal sins in kind and number committed since your last confession.
3. You must resolve to amend your life.

In the Bible: Romans 8:17; Romans 3:23–26
In the Catechism: CCC 1448

Going Deeper

When we sin we become restless and unhappy. God doesn't want us to be restless and unhappy so he invites us to come to Reconciliation so that he can fill us with his joy. There may be times in your life when you feel far from God. But never think that God doesn't want you to return to him. Never think that your sins are greater than God's love. God's love and mercy will always be waiting for you in the Sacrament of Reconciliation.

102. **Q: What are the three actions required of us in the Sacrament of Reconciliation?**

A: The three actions required of us in the Sacrament of Reconciliation are: repentance, confession of sins to the priest, and the intention to atone for our sins by performing the penance given by the priest.

In the Bible: 1 John 1:9
In the Catechism: CCC 1491

Going Deeper

Regular Reconciliation is one of the most powerful ways that God shares his grace and mercy with us. God asks us to be sorry for our sins, confess them out loud to a priest, and do an act of penance so that our friendship with God can be restored and strengthened. The more you go to Reconciliation the more you will come to realize the incredible power of God's grace and mercy in your life.

103. Q: Who has the power to forgive sin?

A: Jesus Christ through a Catholic priest.

In the Bible: John 20:23; 2 Corinthians 5:18
In the Catechism: CCC 1461, 1493, 1495

104. Q: Can the priest talk about your sins with other people?

A: No. The priest must keep secret all sins confessed to him.

In the Bible: 2 Corinthians 5:18–19
In the Catechism: CCC 1467

Going Deeper

If you are nervous about going to Confession, it's ok. Being nervous is natural. Just know that the priest is there to help you. He will not think poorly of you because of your sins or tell anyone what they are. Instead, he will be happy that you went to Confession. Remember, the priest is there to encourage you, extend God's love and mercy to you, and to help you grow in virtue.

105. Q: What is the purpose of penance?

A: After you have confessed your sins, the priest will propose penance for you to perform. The purpose of these acts of penance is to repair the harm caused by sin and to re-establish the habits of a disciple of Christ.

In the Bible: Luke 19:8; Acts 2:38
In the Catechism: CCC 1459–1460

Going Deeper

Friendship is beautiful but it is also fragile. God gives us the Sacrament of Reconciliation to heal the pain caused by sin and to repair our friendship with him. When we do our penance we show God that we are truly sorry. Penance helps our souls get healthy again.

106. **Q: How often should you go to Confession?**

A: You should go immediately if you are in a state of mortal sin; otherwise, it is recommended to go once a month because it is highly recommended to confess venial sins. Prior to confession you should carefully examine your conscience.

In the Bible: Acts 3:19; Luke 5:31–32; Jeremiah 31:19
In the Catechism: CCC 1457, 1458

Going Deeper

God loves healthy relationships and forgiveness is essential to having healthy relationships. Regularly going to God in the Sacrament of Reconciliation and asking for forgiveness is a powerful way to have a fabulous relationship with God. Many of the saints went to Reconciliation every month, some even more often. They knew that going to Confession was the only way to be reconciled to God. They also knew that nothing brought them more joy than having a strong friendship with Jesus.

107. **Q: Does the Sacrament of Reconciliation reconcile us only with God?**

A: No. The Sacrament of Reconciliation reconciles us with God and with the Church.

In the Bible: 1 Corinthians 12:26
In the Catechism: CCC 1422, 1449, 1469

Going Deeper

God delights in his relationship with you and he delights in your relationship with the Church. Sin makes your soul sick, it hurts other people, and it harms your relationship with God and the Church. When we go to Confession, God forgives us and heals our soul. He also heals our relationship with him and with the Church through the Sacrament of Reconciliation.

108. **Q: How do we experience God's mercy?**

A: We experience God's mercy in the Sacrament of Reconciliation. We also experience God's mercy through the kindness, generosity, and compassion of other people. God's mercy always draws us closer to him. We can also be instruments of God's mercy by exercising the works of mercy with kindness, generosity, and compassion.

In the Bible: Luke 3:11; John 8:11
In the Catechism: CCC 1422, 1449, 2447

Going Deeper

Sometimes when we do something that is wrong we may be tempted to think that God will not love us anymore. But that is never true. God will always love you because our God is a merciful God. God shows us his mercy by forgiving us, teaching us, and caring for our physical and spiritual needs even when we don't deserve it. He shows us his mercy through the Sacrament of Reconciliation and through the loving actions of other people. God invites you to spread his mercy by forgiving others, praying for others, and caring for those in need.

109. **Q: Where in the Church building is Jesus present in a special way?**

A: In the tabernacle.

In the Bible: Exodus 40:34; Luke 22:19
In the Catechism: CCC 1379

110. **Q: Who is the source of all blessings?**

A: God is the source of all blessings. In the Mass we praise and adore God the Father as the source of every blessing in creation. We also thank God the Father for sending us his Son. Most of all we express our gratitude to God the Father for making us his children.

In the Bible: Luke 1:68–79; Psalm 72:18–19
In the Catechism: CCC 1083, 1110

Going Deeper

You are blessed in so many ways. But every blessing comes from the very first blessing—life! God has given you life and made you his child. This is an incredible blessing! One of the greatest ways we can show God our gratitude is by going to Mass. By showing up every Sunday and participating in Mass, you show God how thankful you are for everything he has done for you.

111. **Q: True or False. When you receive Holy Communion, you receive a piece of bread that signifies, symbolizes, or represents Jesus.**

A: False.

In the Bible: Matthew 26:26
In the Catechism: CCC 1374, 1413

112. **Q: What do you receive in Holy Communion?**

A: The Body, Blood, Soul, and Divinity of Christ.

In the Bible: 1 Corinthians 11:24 ; John 6: 54–55
In the Catechism: CCC 1374, 1413

Going Deeper

Jesus is truly present in the Eucharist. It is not a symbol; it is Jesus. We receive all of Jesus in the Eucharist. Even the tiniest crumb that falls from the wafer contains all of Jesus. The bread and wine become Jesus at the moment of Consecration. This is an incredible moment. In this moment Jesus comes among us once again. Every time you go to Mass, bread and wine are transformed into the Body and Blood of Jesus. You are blessed to be able to receive Jesus in the Eucharist.

113. **Q: What is Transubstantiation?**

A: Transubstantiation is when the bread and wine become the Body and Blood of Jesus.

In the Bible: Matthew 26:26; Mark 14:22; Luke 22:19–20
In the Catechism: CCC 1376

Going Deeper

God has the power to transform everyone and everything he comes in contact with. Everyday, in every Catholic Church, during every Mass, God transforms ordinary bread and wine into the Body and Blood of Jesus Christ. After receiving Jesus in the Eucharist, many of the saints prayed that they would become what they had received. God answered their prayers and transformed their lives by helping them to live like Jesus. Just like with the saints, God can transform your life. Every time you receive Jesus in the Eucharist worthily, you can become a little more like him. Just like Jesus, you can love generously and serve powerfully everyone you meet.

114. **Q: When does the bread and wine change into the Body and Blood of Christ?**

A: It is changed by the words and intention of the priest at the moment of Consecration during Mass. The priest, asking for the help of the Holy Spirit, says the same words Jesus said at the Last Supper: "This is my body which will be given up for you... This is the cup of my blood..."

In the Bible: Mark 14:22; Luke 22:19–20
In the Catechism: CCC 1412, 1413

Going Deeper

The Last Supper is the most famous meal in the history of the world. In that room two thousand years ago, Jesus gave himself completely to his apostles. Every time we come to Mass, the priest recites the same words as Jesus during the Last Supper. When he does, the wheat bread and grape wine become the Body and Blood of Jesus. Amazing! Jesus wants to give himself completely to you just as he gave himself completely to his apostles at the Last Supper. Jesus wants to be invited into your life. He wants to encourage you, guide you, listen to you, and love you. He offers himself to you in a special way at Mass, especially in the amazing gift of Holy Communion.

115. **Q: What are the benefits of receiving the Body and Blood of Jesus in the Eucharist?**

A: When you receive Jesus in the Eucharist you become more united with the Lord, your venial sins are forgiven, and you are given grace to avoid grave sins. Receiving Jesus in the Eucharist also increases your love for Jesus and reinforces the fact that you are a member of God's family — the Catholic Church.

In the Bible: John 6:56–57
In the Catechism: CCC 1391–1396

Going Deeper

The Eucharist empowers us to do great things for God. The saints did incredible things for God throughout their lives and the Eucharist was the source of their strength. Through Holy Communion we grow closer to God, move further away from sinful habits, and grow in love for Jesus and the Catholic Church. The Eucharist is the ultimate food for your soul and it will give you the strength and courage to serve God and others powerfully just like the saints.

116. **Q: How important is the Eucharist to the life of the Church?**

A: The Eucharist is indispensable in the life of the Church. The Eucharist is the heart of the Church. One of the reasons the Eucharist is so important to the life of the Church is because, through it, Jesus unites every member of the Church with his sacrifice on the cross. Every grace that flows from Jesus' suffering, death, and Resurrection comes to us through the Church.

In the Bible: John 6:51, 54, 56
In the Catechism: CCC 1324, 1331, 1368, 1407

Going Deeper

Jesus promised to be with us always, no matter what. He has been keeping this promise for over 2,000 years. Jesus is always with us in the Eucharist. The Eucharist unites us to Jesus and his Church. It also unites us to one another. We are blessed to have the Eucharist. Only through the Catholic Church can we receive the gift of the Eucharist. We are blessed to be Catholic.

117. **Q: Should you receive Holy Communion in the state of mortal sin?**

A: No. If you do, you commit the additional mortal sin of sacrilege.

In the Bible: 1 Corinthians 11:27–29
In the Catechism: CCC 1385, 1415, 1457

Going Deeper

If Jesus came to visit your home and it was so messy you couldn't open the door to let Jesus in, that would be terrible. No matter how much Jesus wants to be a part of our lives he will never force himself upon us. Mortal sin slams the door of our souls in Jesus' face. It breaks our relationship with God and prevents the wonderful graces of the Eucharist from flowing into our hearts, minds, and souls. Reconciliation reopens the door to our souls and let's Jesus enter our lives again.

118. **Q: What is sacrilege?**

A: It is the abuse of a sacred person, place, or thing.

In the Bible: 1 Corinthians 11:27–29
In the Catechism: CCC 2120

119. **Q: If you are in a state of mortal sin, what should you do before receiving Holy Communion?**

A: You should go to Confession as soon as possible.

In the Bible: 2 Corinthians 5:20
In the Catechism: CCC 1385, 1457

120. **Q: Who offered the first Mass?**

A: Jesus Christ.

> In the Bible: Mark 14:22–24
> In the Catechism: CCC 1323

121. **Q: When did Jesus offer the first Mass?**

A: On Holy Thursday night, the night before He died, at the Last Supper.

> In the Bible: Matthew 26:26–28
> In the Catechism: CCC 1323

122. **Q: Who offers the Eucharistic sacrifice?**

A: Jesus is the eternal high priest. In the Mass, he offers the Eucharistic sacrifice through the ministry of the priest.

> In the Bible: Mark 14:22; Matthew 26:26; Luke 22:19; 1 Corinthians 11:24;
> In the Catechism: CCC 1348

Going Deeper

The Last Supper was the first Eucharistic celebration. This was the apostles First Communion, and the first time anybody had ever received the Eucharist. The Mass is not just a symbol of what happened that night. Jesus is truly present in the Eucharist. Every time we receive Holy Communion Jesus gives himself to us in the same way he gave himself to his apostles over 2,000 years ago. Jesus works through the priest at Mass to transform the bread and wine into his Body and Blood.

123. **Q: What is the Sacrifice of the Mass?**

A: It is the sacrifice of Jesus Christ on Calvary, the memorial of Christ's Passover, made present when the priest repeats the words of Consecration spoken by Jesus over the bread and wine at the Last Supper.

> In the Bible: Hebrews 7:25–27
> In the Catechism: CCC 1364, 1413

Going Deeper

God loves you so much and he will go to unimaginable lengths to prove his love for you. On Good Friday Jesus was beaten, bullied, mocked, spat upon, cursed at, and crucified on the cross. Jesus laid down his life for us. On Easter Sunday Jesus rose from the dead. He did this so that we might live a very different life while here on earth and happily with him forever in heaven. Every time we go to Mass we remember the life of Jesus, the path he invites us to walk, and the incredible lengths he went to show us his love.

124. **Q: Who can preside at the Eucharist?**

A: Only an ordained priest can preside at the Eucharist and Consecrate the bread and the wine so that they become the Body and Blood of Jesus.

In the Bible: John 13:3–8
In the Catechism: CCC 1411

Going Deeper

To be a priest is a great honor and privilege. Priests lay down their lives to serve God and his people. The priesthood is a life of service. One of the ultimate privileges of the priesthood is standing in Jesus' place and transforming bread and wine into the Eucharist. This privilege is reserved for priests alone. Nobody other than a priest can do this.

125. **Q: How do we participate in the Sacrifice of the Mass?**

A: By uniting ourselves and our intentions to the bread and wine, offered by the priest, which become Jesus' sacrifice to the Father.

In the Bible: Romans 12:1
In the Catechism: CCC 1407

126. **Q: What does the Eucharistic celebration we participate in at Mass always include?**

A: The Eucharist celebration always includes: the proclamation of the Word of God; thanksgiving to God the Father for all his blessings; the Consecration of the bread and wine; and participation in the liturgical banquet by receiving the Lord's Body and Blood. These elements constitute one single act of worship.

In the Bible: Luke 24:13–35
In the Catechism: CCC 1345–1355, 1408

Going Deeper

The Mass follows a certain formula that is always repeated and never changes. You could go to Mass anywhere in the world and you will always find it is the same. At every Mass we read from the Bible, show God our gratitude for the blessing of Jesus, witness bread and wine transformed into the Body and Blood of Jesus, and receive Jesus during Holy Communion. In the midst of this great routine, God wants to surprise you. You could spend a lifetime going to Mass every single day and at the end of your life still be surprised by what God has to say to you in the Mass. The Mass is truly amazing!

127. **Q: What role does music play in the Mass?**

A: Sacred music helps us to worship God.

In the Bible: Ps 57:8–10; Ephesians 5:19; Hebrews 2:12; Colossians 3:16;
In the Catechism: CCC 1156

Going Deeper

Sometimes when we are praying it can be difficult to find the right words to express how we feel. To help us, God gives us the great gift of sacred music. Over the course of the Mass there will be songs of praise, songs of worship, songs of petition, and songs of thanksgiving. Sacred music helps raise our hearts to God and bond us together as a community calling out to God with one voice.

128. **Q: What is the Lord's Day?**

A: Sunday is the Lord's Day. It is a day of rest. It is a day to gather as a family. It is the principal day for celebrating the Eucharist because it is the day of the Resurrection.

In the Bible: Exodus 31:15; Matthew 28:1; Mark 16:2; John 20:1;
In the Catechism: CCC 1166; 1193; 2174

Going Deeper

Sunday is a very special day. The Resurrection of Jesus is so important that we celebrate it every day at Mass. But we celebrate the Resurrection of Jesus in a special way every Sunday. We do that by resting, spending time with family, and going to Mass. The Lord's Day is a day to marvel at all the amazing ways God has blessed us, and because of that it is a day of gratitude.

129. Q: Is it a mortal sin for you to miss Mass on Sunday or a Holy Day through your own fault?

A: Yes.

> In the Bible: Exodus 20:8
> In the Catechism: CCC 2181

130. Q: **Which person of the Holy Trinity do you receive in Confirmation?**

A: The Holy Spirit.

> In the Bible: Romans 8:15
> In the Catechism: CCC 1302

131. Q: **What happens in the Sacrament of Confirmation?**

A: The Holy Spirit comes upon us and strengthens us to be soldiers of Christ that we may spread and defend the Catholic faith.

> In the Bible: John 14:26; 15:26
> In the Catechism: CCC 1303, 2044

132. Q: **What is Confirmation?**

A: Confirmation is a Sacrament that perfects Baptismal grace. Through it we receive the Holy Spirit and are strengthened in grace so we can grow in virtue, live holy lives, and carry out the mission God calls us to.

> In the Bible: John 20:22; Acts 2:1–4
> In the Catechism: CCC: 1285, 1316

Going Deeper

When you are older you will be blessed to receive the Sacrament of Confirmation. Confirmation reminds us that in Baptism God blessed us with a special mission and filled us with the Holy Spirit. Through an outpouring of the Holy Spirit at Confirmation, we are filled with the courage and wisdom to live out the mission God has given us. Confirmation deepens our friendship with Jesus and the Catholic Church. It reminds us that we are sons and daughters of a great King. It will be a special moment in your life and a wonderful blessing!

133. **Q: When is Confirmation received?**

A: Most Catholics in the West receive Confirmation during their teenage years, but in the East Confirmation is administered immediately after Baptism.

In the Bible: Hebrews 6:1–3
In the Catechism: CCC 1306, 1318

Going Deeper

Baptism, Confirmation and First Holy Communion are called the Sacraments of Initiation. In a special way, the Sacraments of Initiation deepen our friendship with Jesus and the Church, fill us with what we need to live out God's mission for our lives, and inspire us to become all that God created us to be. It is important to remember that these three Sacraments are connected. They are the foundation for a fabulous friendship with God on earth and forever in heaven. In some parts of the world, and at different times throughout history, people have received these Sacraments at different times according to local traditions and practical considerations. For example, hundreds of years ago, the bishop may have only visited a village once every two or three years, and so Confirmation would take place when he visited. Even today, some children receive Baptism, First Communion, and Confirmation all at the same time.

134. **Q: What are the Seven Gifts of the Holy Spirit?**

A: Wisdom, understanding, counsel, fortitude, knowledge, piety, and fear of the Lord.

In the Bible: Isaiah 11:2–3
In the Catechism: CCC 1830, 1831

135. **Q: Before you are confirmed, you will promise the bishop that you will never give up the practice of your Catholic faith for anyone or anything. Did you ever make that promise before?**

A: Yes, at Baptism.

In the Bible: Joshua 24:21–22
In the Catechism: CCC 1298

136. **Q: Most of you were baptized as little babies. How could you make that promise?**

A: Our parents and godparents made that promise for us.

In the Bible: Mark 16:16
In the Catechism: CCC 1253

137. **Q: What kind of sin is it to receive Confirmation in the state of mortal sin?**
    A: A sacrilege.

    > In the Bible: 1 Corinthians 11:27–29
    > In the Catechism: CCC 2120

138. **Q: If you have committed mortal sin, what should you do before receiving Confirmation?**
    A: You should make a good Confession.

    > In the Bible: 2 Corinthians 5:20; Luke 15:18
    > In the Catechism: CCC 1310

139. **Q: What are the three traditional vocations?**
    A: Married life, Holy Orders, and the consecrated life.

    > In the Bible: Ephesians 5:31–32; Hebrews 5:6, 7:11; Ps 110:4; Matthew 19:12; 1 Corinthians 7:34–66
    > In the Catechism: CCC 914, 1536, 1601

140. **Q: What are the three vows that a consecrated man or woman takes?**
    A: Chastity, Poverty, and Obedience.

    > In the Bible: Matthew 19:21; Matthew 19:12; 1 Corinthians 7:34–36; Hebrews 10:7;
    > In the Catechism: CCC 915

141. **Q: What are the three ranks (degrees) of Holy Orders?**
    A: Deacon, Priest, and Bishop.

    > In the Bible: 1 Timothy 4:14; 2 Timothy 1:6–7
    > In the Catechism: CCC 1554

142. **Q: For whom did God make marriage?**
    A: One man and one woman.

    > In the Bible: Genesis 1:26–28; Ephesians 5:31
    > In the Catechism: CCC 1601, 2360

143. **Q: Is it possible for two men or two women to get married?**

A: No.

> In the Bible: Genesis 19:1–29; Romans 1:24–27; 1 Corinthians 6:9;
> In the Catechism: CCC 2357, 2360

144. **Q: When can a man and woman begin living together?**

A: Only after their marriage.

> In the Bible: 1 Corinthians 6:18–20
> In the Catechism: CCC 235

145. **Q: What are the three marriage promises a husband and wife make to each other?**

A: Faithfulness, permanence, and being open to having children.

> In the Bible: Matthew 19:6; Genesis 1:28
> In the Catechism: CCC 1640, 1641, 1664

146. **Q: Why is abortion wrong?**

A: Because it takes the life of a baby in its mother's womb.

> In the Bible: Jeremiah 1:5; Psalm 139:13
> In the Catechism: CCC 2270

147. **Q: How many commandments are there?**

A: Ten.

> In the Bible: Exodus 20:1–18; Deuteronomy 5:6–21
> In the Catechism: CCC 2054

148. **Q: What are the Ten Commandments?**

A: 1. I, the Lord, am your God. You shall not have other gods besides me.
2. You shall not take the name of the Lord, your God, in vain.
3. Remember to keep holy the Lord's Day.
4. Honor your father and mother.
5. You shall not kill.
6. You shall not commit adultery.
7. You shall not steal.
8. You shall not bear false witness against your neighbor.
9. You shall not covet your neighbor's wife.
10. You shall not covet your neighbor's goods.

In the Bible: Exodus 20:1–18; Deuteronomy 5:6–21
In the Catechism: CCC 496, 497

149. Q: **What are the four main kinds of prayer?**

A: The four main kinds of prayer are adoration, thanksgiving, petition, and intercession.

In the Bible: Ps 95:6; Colossians 4:2; James 5:16; 1 John 3:22
In the Catechism: CCC 2628, 2629, 2634, 2638, 2639

150. Q: **How often should we pray?**

A: Every day.

In the Bible: 1 Thessalonians 5:17; Luke 18:1
In the Catechism: CCC 2742

Acknowledgments

This project began with a dream: to create the best First Reconciliation and First Communion experience in the world. For the millions of young souls that will experience this program we hope we have delivered on that dream.

Hundreds of people have poured their time, talent, and expertise into *Blessed*. It is the result of years of research, development, and testing. To everyone who has contributed—and you know who you are—in every stage of the process: Thank You! May God bless you and reward you richly for your generosity.

Special thanks to: Jack Beers, Allen and Anita Hunt, Bridget Eichold, Father Robert Sherry, Steve Lawson, Shawna Navaro, Ben Skudlarek, Katie Ferrara, and Mark Moore.

Beyond the enormous talent contributions, others have been incredibly generous with their money. *Blessed* was funded by a group of incredibly generous donors. It will now be made available at no cost to every parish in North America. This is one of the many ways that this program is unique.

Everything great in history has been accomplished by people who believed that the future could be better than the past. Thank you for believing!

Now we offer *Blessed* to the Church as a gift, hopeful that it will help young Catholics encounter Jesus and discover the genius of Catholicism.

Blessed was:

Written by: Matthew Kelly
Illustrated by: Carolina Farias
Designed by: The Dynamic Catholic Design Team.
Principal designers: Ben Hawkins and Jenny Miller

Help *Blessed* become The-Best-Version-of-Itself

Blessed is different from other programs in a hundred ways. One way that it is different is that it is always changing and improving. We need your help with this. Whether you find a typo or think of some fun way to improve the program, please email us and tell us about it so that year after year Blessed can become even more dynamic.

blessed@dynamiccatholic.com

Blessed

The Dynamic Catholic First Reconciliation Experience
©2017 The Dynamic Catholic Institute and Matthew Kelly

ISBN 978-1-63582-019-5

FIRST EDITION

{ To re-energize the Catholic Church in America by developing world-class resources that inspire people to rediscover the genius of Catholicism. }

{ To be the innovative leader in the New Evangelization helping Catholics and their parishes become the-best-version-of-themselves. }

Blessed is part of

THE CATHOLIC MOMENTS SERIES

10 programs we believe will re-energize the Catholic Church in America. If you would like to learn more about The Catholic Moments Series or get involved in our work, visit *DynamicCatholic.com*.

CONFIRMATION

LENT AND EASTER

ADVENT AND CHRISTMAS

FIRST COMMUNION

FIRST RECONCILIATION

MARRIAGE PREP

BIRTH AND BAPTISM

RITE OF CHRISTIAN
INITIATION FOR ADULTS

DAILY PRAYER

SUNDAY MASS

DEATH AND DYING